LEGENDS & LORE
OF
SOMERSET COUNTY

KNITTING BETTY, THE GREAT SWAMP DEVIL
& MORE TALES FROM CENTRAL NEW JERSEY

MICHAEL HAYNES

Charleston   London

THE
History
PRESS

Published by The History Press
Charleston, SC 29403
www.historypress.net

Copyright © 2014 by Michael Haynes
All rights reserved

Front cover, top: Courtesy of Abby Berenbak.

First published 2014

Manufactured in the United States

ISBN 978.1.62619.679.7

Library of Congress CIP data applied for.

This book is for Mary Christina Haynes

CONTENTS

PART III: THE WEIRD STUFF

ACKNOWLEDGEMENTS

Stories do not happen without people, and there are many people I'm indebted to for helping me discover these stories. First and foremost, I would like to thank Jack Rushing of the Great Swamp Folklore Project, one of the greatest folklorists of the twenty-first century, for introducing me to the great river of the oral tradition of New Jersey. I would like to thank renowned psychic Jane Dougherty, who, for better or worse, opened the supernatural door for me onto the other side of existence. And I cannot forget to thank Mark Moran and Mark Sceurman, publishers of the greatest magazine on the planet, *Weird NJ*, in which some of these stories originally appeared.

On a more personal note, my gratitude goes to my best friend and fellow explorer of New Jersey, Charles Kelemen, without whose intelligence, insight and friendship these tales would have remained fragmented vignettes. I also want to acknowledge the contributions of my late father, Arthur Haynes, whose own love of history was transferred to me and who was also the first person to introduce me to the significance of all those places contained herein. But most of all I want to thank the greatest love of my life, my wife, Mary Christina Haynes, the girl from Kentucky whom I brought into this state, who embraced its wonder and weirdness and whose love, encouragement and dedication gave me the strength and endurance to write this book.

INTRODUCTION

First, I'll tell you what I'm not. I'm not a ghost hunter or paranormal investigator. I'm not a psychic, sensitive or intuitive. I claim no such abilities or talents in fields outside our present scientific and academic knowledge. What I claim is a profound dedication to history and a deep love of stories. It was these dual motivations that sent me on a lifelong quest to learn the story of our great state of New Jersey. They were not the motivations behind discovering the ghosts, monsters and other strange phenomena that populate some of those stories. In fact, encountering them was both accidental and incidental to my research, but much to my surprise, I discovered that they were an essential element to our past and will not be denied recognition. The tales contained in this book are ones that I've collected or experienced myself from years of exploring the history of the great state of my birth.

To my knowledge, most of these stories have never been taken out of the oral tradition. Some have, but they are either in disconnected anecdotes or transformed into versions unrecognizable from their origins. Some you might never have heard or read before. Some you might have encountered but in different versions; that's just the nature of the oral tradition. These stories are presented to you the way I first encountered them. I have made every attempt to be as honest, faithful and rational in my reporting of them as possible. I present them not to convince you of their veracity, but to give you a glimpse into the vast, rich, weird and wonderful culture of New Jersey.

No one story will convince anybody of a strange event, and frankly, it shouldn't. Part of the reason an event is called "supernatural" is that it's not

OUTLINE MAP OF

HUNTERDON & SOMERSET

COUNTIES

An 1881 map
of Somerset and
Hunterdon Counties.
From History of
Hunterdon and
Somerset Counties,
New Jersey, *1881.*

testable by scientific methods and hypotheses. That doesn't mean that in the future it won't be provable, but until someone can come up with an $E = mc^2$–type equation to explain the continuance of consciousness after death or the existence of our cryptids and strange lights, those events will have to remained unexplained. Although this volume contains just a fraction of tales I've collected through my life, these stories were chosen not just for their intrinsic value but also because they have happened or still occur in public locales. You are completely free to go to these places and investigate for yourself without trespassing on or violating anyone's privacy. If something strange happens to you while you're there, or if you discover another reason behind these events, that would be terrific. If you find nothing odd, well, that happens to me 99 percent of the time when I visit these places, too. However, I will say that for 100 percent of the locations I've been to, I haven't found them a waste of time. I hope you'll find the same.

New Jersey has been the home for many of the incredible achievements and breakthroughs that have given us the civilization we know today. It is also the home of the many legends and monsters that haunt the human imagination. We may not always see the connection between these two facets of ourselves, we may even think that they are contrary to each other, but imagination and achievement, fueled by curiosity, is what drives humanity. We are privileged to live on this little strange and beautiful patch of land on planet Earth where all that comes together.

PART I
GHOSTS

1
CHINQUEKA

CHIMNEY ROCK, BRIDGEWATER TOWNSHIP

Located at the apex of the First Watchung Mountain, Chimney Rock Park in Bridgewater Township, Somerset County, has served as a spectacular lookout on the Raritan Valley for as long as humans have occupied New Jersey. On especially clear days, you can see from the Atlantic Highlands in the southeast to the Delaware Valley in the southwest—in other words, the entire middle span of our great state. Centuries before it would become central New Jersey, though, that view would be the last thing that a young Native American woman would see—at least while she was alive.

We don't know how far back in time her story begins. Like most Native American peoples, the Lenapes didn't track time in the obsessive chronological order that Westerners do. It will have to suffice that the tale begins before 1524, which was when Europeans first saw the future Garden State. In those times, the Lenapes had established five villages along the Raritan River in present-day Bound Brook that were ruled by a single king. The story handed down to us tells of a hunting trip that the king and his men took into the Ramapo Mountains of northeastern New Jersey one season. There they encountered another hunting party led by a prince of the Manhattan tribe. Both parties decided to hunt together, and the king got along so well with the prince that, at the end of the hunt, he decided to betroth his daughter, Chinqueka (which in Algonquian means "goldfinch"), to the prince and invited him back to the villages at Bound Brook. It didn't bother the king that he had already betrothed Chinqueka to a local Lenape warrior named Manassamitt.

The view from Chimney Rock, Bridgewater. This would have been the last sight Chinqueka saw while alive. *Author's collection.*

Chimney Rock, sight of the Manhattan prince's murder at the hands of Manassamitt. His body was thrown into the ravine below the cliff. *Author's collection.*

Of course, the decision to marry Chinqueka to the prince wasn't the king's alone. As a matrilineal society, it was the leading Lenape women who held the ultimate decision since they controlled the influence, power and bloodlines of the nation. In fact, it was they who appointed the king to his post in the first place and could have withdrawn him from his position at any time had they

thought that he wasn't doing his job right. Upon meeting the prince, however, the female elders agreed with the king that the prince was a better match for Chinqueka than Manassamitt, and they allowed the wedding to proceed.

This change in fiancés didn't bother Chinqueka, either, because she fell in love with the prince at first sight. During the days after the hunting party returned and the preparations for the wedding were being made, Chinqueka and the prince would go high above the villages to Chimney Rock for some alone time, not unlike hundreds of Bridgewater-Raritan High School alumni do centuries later. One day, the prince arrived early and, finding himself alone, decided to wait there for Chinqueka. However, he wasn't as alone as he thought, for hiding nearby was the jilted warrior who had been Chinqueka's first fiancé. Manassamitt caught the prince by surprise, clubbed his head to a bloody pulp, threw his body over the cliff into the ravine where Chimney Rock Road now runs and made his escape. When she finally arrived, Chinqueka saw the evidence of the murder, surmised what had happened and threw herself off Chimney Rock to join the prince in the afterlife.

The story doesn't tell us what happened to Manassamitt, but it goes on to reveal that the Manhattans went to war with the Lenapes over the murder of the prince for several years afterward. It also tells us that Chinqueka was unable to be with him after death, for vague stories of seeing and hearing a weeping Lenape woman have been reported at Chimney Rock since then. Though I've never seen or heard Chinqueka myself while at Chimney Rock, I have to wonder if she wasn't responsible for a discovery I made there years ago that is still with me today. Before I get to that, let me tell you a little more about the history of Chimney Rock.

Over a century after European colonists arrived in the Raritan Valley, no Lenape of Chinqueka's time would have recognized his homeland. The wigwam villages of Bound Brook had long been buried beneath timber-frame homes and barns; the paths leading through the dense forests had been turned into wide, dirt-covered stage routes; and even the forest itself had been cleared to make way for farmland. The only remnant of the forest now existed along the top ridge of the Watchung Mountains, which had been transformed into lots where the colonists went for their firewood. Chimney Rock had become one of those wood lots, but its commanding view of the Raritan Valley held significance because it was used as a Continental army observation and signal post during the American Revolution. There, a forty-foot-high beacon tower had been constructed by the Continentals, one of twenty-four such towers stretching from White Plains, New York, to Newcastle, Delaware, that were used as a rapid-signaling system in response to British movements. Under the command of General "Mad" Anthony Wayne of the Pennsylvania Line, Chimney Rock also became the prime defensive position for the Continental army during its winter encampment of 1778–79 at Middlebrook, which was literally a few hundred yards below the promontory. There were also three stone huts constructed at Chimney Rock that predated the Revolution and were used by the woodsmen. The huts lie just to the west of the fort; if the leaves don't cover them, you can still walk into the hut foundations and check out the flint blanks in the tiny fireplaces.

Since the signal tower was constructed of wood, nothing of it now remains. It was used on several occasions during the war, although Chimney Rock was not permanently occupied by the Continental army. In fact, in 1778, British lieutenant John Graves Simpcoe of the Queen's Rangers (a unit of disaffected Tories who acted more like war criminals than soldiers) led a raid to Chimney Rock in hopes of capturing General Wayne, but Mad Anthony had given him the slip. Later that night, Simpcoe was captured himself by the residents of Bound Brook and nearly beaten to death, but he was later returned to the British in a prisoner exchange.

In the spring of 1996, my friend Charles Kelemen and I went to Chimney Rock to explore the post and stone huts. Afterward, we had just decided to walk to the nearby reservoir when we simultaneously noticed a bright flash of yellow light on the ridge just above us. At the top of the ridge we saw an old-growth oak tree that had fallen during the winter storms but no obvious source for that flash of light. We decided to climb the escarpment anyway. When we got to the fallen oak, we found some beer cans and trash nearby, but this litter was actually in a hollow in the ground and out of our line of sight from the trail. Having seen enough teenage detritus in our time, we turned to the base of the oak tree, and there, embedded in one of its roots, Charlie spotted a pale pink opal about three-quarters of an inch in diameter. The wood had rotted enough that pulling out the stone was very easy, and I could instantly tell that it had been polished and worked on since one side was flattened as if it had once been attached to an article of clothing or

Possible Lenape opal found by the author at Chimney Rock, 1996. *Author's collection.*

jewelry. However, it was still too dull in luster to have caused the light that drew us to it in the first place. I also knew that since it was embedded in the root that it had to have been in the ground before the tree was there, and this oak had to have been a couple of centuries old when it fell. I offered it to Charlie since he first saw it, but having a bad family history with a previous opal, he wanted nothing to do with it. So I put it my pocket and we went on exploring.

For the next several years, the opal joined my small collection of artifacts from New Jersey history; I normally take only pictures from the sites I visit, but no one was going to miss a stone of small monetary value that had been buried beneath an oak tree for centuries. From time to time, though, I had the idea of giving the opal to a few of the women whom I had been dating since it was the only artifact I had connected with a love story. However, each time I was about to give it away, something negative would happen to the relationship—an argument, a stand-up, a break-up. It was as if something was telling me, "You're not giving it to that one." I was beginning to think that Charlie was on to something about opals being cursed. In 2001 (five years after discovering the stone), I attempted to give it to the woman I was seeing at the time, Mary Christina Wilson, and actually succeeded in placing the opal into her hand, which was a lot further than I got with the previous girlfriends. Christina and I have been together for the last thirteen years. She even had the opal with her on our wedding day.

I don't know if the opal was originally Chinqueka's. Whether it's a local stone or came to New Jersey through the vast trade routes of pre-Columbian North America I don't know, either. I like to think that it did belong to Chinqueka and that it was meant to be in Christina's possession all these years later. Early on in our relationship, Christina got so angry with me that she said she threw the opal in the garbage, only to find it later resting on her dresser! These days, I try my best not to get her angry with me because she is the best thing to ever happen in my life. Perhaps someday, though, centuries from now, some other history nerd will find the opal in the ruins of our house and give it to someone he or she loves, too. I kind of think that's its purpose.

2

THE DEAD RIVER WITCH

LIBERTY CORNER, BERNARDS TOWNSHIP

For the most densely populated state in the country, it's ironic that New Jersey contains many famous trees, and quite a number of them still live in Somerset County. Most are not hard to find. The oldest is the Great Swamp Oak, a seven-hundred-year-old tree standing in the middle of the Lord Stirling Environmental Center in Basking Ridge. Nearby, just off White Bridge Road, is the Daughter of the Swamp Oak, a three-hundred-year-old oak that marks the site of the nineteenth-century ruins of the only Episcopalian-Lutheran church ever to exist. Of course, anyone driving through the middle of Basking Ridge itself can't help but see the Presbyterian Oak, which has been dated to at least half a millennium, in the churchyard. Farther afield is the great oak in Bound Brook, where on July 6, 1776, firebrand Patriot Heindrich Fisher first read the Declaration of Independence to the residents of Somerset County. However, not all our trees have such benevolent reputations. In fact, one of them in Liberty Corner, Bernards Township, had such a terrorizing reputation that it is no longer there.

Long before the first colonist, John Annin, established a trading post there in 1731, the area that would become Liberty Corner was home to three Lenape villages located near the banks of the Dead River. In one of these villages, beneath a giant black walnut tree along the riverbank, lived a Lenape medicine woman whose name has been lost to time. It was said that she was a beautiful young woman who wore a striking, multicolored shawl patterned after a rainbow. Her activities while alive are unknown,

Liberty Corner, Bernards, was once the site of the Lenape village where the Dead River Witch lived. *Author's collection.*

although, in general, Lenape medicine women dealt with the physical aspects of medicine while the men concentrated on the spiritual side of it. After her death, though, the villagers continued to see her around the tree and riverbank she inhabited while living. As the tree grew, its trunk formed a gigantic chasm, large enough for a person to fit into. But more strangely, those who wandered too close to the tree were never seen again. Wisely, the Lenapes started to avoid that spot and gave her spirit a name that has come down to us as the Dead River Witch. Unfortunately for one little girl, the legend would prove itself all too true well into the modern era.

In the autumn of 1853, John Maddock of Burslem, Stratfordshire, England, brought his wife and nine-year-old daughter, Martha, to Liberty Corner. Maddock was not the ordinary, working-class immigrant recently arrived in America but nevertheless had an American dream that could have changed the economic landscape of New Jersey. He was the successful owner of a porcelain factory in England; in fact, his hometown of Burslem was one of six communities in Stratfordshire dedicated to manufacturing porcelain for the growing middle class in America (you can still find examples of his work on the Internet). Maddock's dream was to establish a porcelain factory in the United States, and in Liberty Corner he must have thought he found the perfect place. Not only located between his two biggest markets of New York and Philadelphia, Somerset County also contained the raw material in its rocks to make the high-quality teacups and dinner plates he was renowned for. All it lacked were skilled artisans and the vision to make Liberty Corner a center of stoneware artistry on par with those in England. However, a darker force from New Jersey's past would stop that dream from coming true.

Martha Maddock's tombstone in the Liberty Corner Presbyterian Churchyard. While the tombstone was erected after her disappearance, there is no body buried beneath it. *Author's collection.*

We don't know if the Maddocks had heard or heeded the story of the Dead River Witch when they arrived in Liberty Corner in 1853, but on November 21, young Martha disappeared from Liberty Corner, never to be seen again. Before she vanished, however, some residents did see her, but not alone. They reported that they saw her walking near the riverbank with a beautiful, dark-skinned woman who was wearing a shawl patterned after a rainbow. The search for Martha or the woman yielded nothing, not a trace of what could have happened to them. Finally, with winter setting in and with the Maddocks believing Martha dead, a memorial was held for her at the Presbyterian Church in town. The tombstone to her memory was erected later in the churchyard, but there is no body lying beneath it.

Heartbroken over the loss of their youngest child, the Maddocks returned to England. John Maddock would eventually become mayor of Burslem and become known for instituting an early form of healthcare insurance for his employees—it makes you wonder what the possibilities for New Jersey and America could have been had his daughter lived. Of course, there are a number of possibilities that could have befallen Martha besides running into the ghost of a Lenape medicine woman to explain her disappearance. The most obvious is that she fell into the Dead River and drowned, her body dragged too far down and away for anyone to recover. There are also a number of hollows to the west of Liberty Corner that

The Witch's Tree on the banks of Dead River in Liberty Corner. The spirits of those captured by the Dead River Witch are reputed to live within the tree. *Photo courtesy of Charles Kelemen.*

would be hard to thoroughly explore. Additionally, the area on the east side of Schley Mountain, at the present location of the Leonard J. Buck Gardens, is now known to be riddled with caverns formed during the ice age that appear and disappear at random; depending on how far Martha could have wandered, she may have accidently stumbled into one of them, which would make finding her impossible. There is, however, one bit of evidence left after 160 years that brings her disappearance back to the Dead River Witch.

In the spring of 2001, my friend Charles Kelemen and I went to Liberty Corner to search for the Witch's Tree. I had known the story of it for almost a decade by then, but though I had grown up only a few miles from Liberty Corner, finding the tree was tricky because the brush along Somerville Road always obscured it. However, on this morning, the underbrush was thinned out, and we had no problem spotting the tree from the road. Pulling over, we got out and walked across a field of knee-high grass to the tree. It was as creepy as legend had it. It was a little farther from the present-day riverbank than I imagined, but even in the morning light, the tortured chasm in the trunk was clearly visible to us. Having my camera with me, I took a picture of the tree. At that instant, I was swarmed in a cloud of black flies. Charlie was engulfed, too, even though he was standing thirty feet to my right. Neither of us got within fifty feet of the tree, and though we wanted to examine it more closely, we both took the swarm of flies as a warning. In fact, they plagued us until we got back into the car.

Upon reviewing the photo after it was developed, I made a weird discovery. I discerned at least three human-like figures on the right side of the trunk. The uppermost figure contains just a head, whereas the lower two contain heads and torsos. Of course, this might be matrixing—seeing patterns where none really exists—on my part, but having spent a lot of time in the west country of the United Kingdom, where this kind of facial phenomena in trees is common, and knowing the legend of the Dead River Witch, I have to wonder if these are not representations of those who disappeared over the centuries. I also have to wonder if Martha's spirit is still with them in that tree.

Since that time, I have been back to Liberty Corner on several occasions, but there have been many changes along Somerville Road. Several office complexes have been built on the road nearby, and now a jogging path runs along the road where the tree was once located. I consider that almost as tragic as what once happened there, but something tells me that the Dead River Witch will not allow herself to fade so easily into modernization.

3
YAGOO

BASKING RIDGE, BERNARDS TOWNSHIP

From the heart of the Great Swamp National Wildlife Refuge, the brackish waters flow down the swamp's rim to form the Passiac River as it makes its meandering way through eastern New Jersey and eventually to the sea. Here the river is not much more than a large stream, flowing from Basking Ridge into the suburban Union County towns of Long Hill, Berkeley Heights and New Providence. But this bucolic setting hides a secret, the kind of secret you at first wouldn't associate with New Jersey. Slavery was as prevalent here as it was in Virginia, the Carolinas and Georgia. Hundreds of men, women and children were stripped of their right to self-determination and forced to carve the wilderness to the wills of their owners. It is the uncomfortable truth that there were slaves in your backyards. Even as time and history tried to erase the memory of their presence, though, many say that their spirits still linger along the river and back into the swamp and that they are led by a man named Yagoo.

Yagoo was born into an African royal family in the mid-seventeenth century, a prince among his people. Who his people were and what they called themselves is no longer known, for they were conquered by a rival tribe and sold to European slavers. This was how many of the nearly 10 million Africans who were enslaved during the four centuries of the global slave trade began their lives of servitude—it is another uncomfortable truth that the hands of the slavers came in all colors. Having survived the Middle Passage, and possibly some ports in the Caribbean colonies, Yagoo arrived in the newly British city of New York, where he became the property of a land speculator who held vast tracts of wilderness near the Great Swamp. Whether his former status as a prince was known or not, Yagoo came to be in charge of three hundred other slaves whose mission was to trek thirty miles west into the colony of East Jersey and "improve" the land there for settlement by white colonists. In other words, they were to clear the land of the primeval trees and their trunks, dislodge the massive glacial stones deposited there from the ice age, dig trenches to drain the marshes and, if any of them survived the backbreaking labor, freezing winters and disease-ridden summers, move on to the next tract and do the same things.

Even with such a large number of people, this was not a short project. With the vast acreage they had to clear, using only axes, ropes and their own backs, they spent years in and around the Great Swamp and Passaic River, long enough for them to become familiar with the territory and long enough for many of them to die there. During that time, they probably learned from the Lenapes and the few colonists who ventured into the area what fauna and flora could be used for food and medicine, established their own community and tried as best as possible to adjust in what must have been a truly alien world from their places of birth. They may have even heard about the community of free Africans and African Americans who were living in Elizabeth Town not far from them to the southeast. The town included several families whose freedom had been purchased by antislavery Quakers and were being taught by the Quakers to live like Western colonists. For some of them, that must have been as equally alien as the North American forests above their heads and the animals lurking about them in the brush, but at least that was a life without chains. Of course, there must always have been the thoughts of escape, but to where? In the sparse settlements, runaway slaves could be easily detected. The unfamiliar wilderness was fraught with even more dangers, and the white colonists kept moving into it, pushing it and the uncertain possibility of escape to it farther out of reach. Day after day, there were trees to be cut, boulders to be moved, food to find and the hope that a stray cut or broken bone wouldn't kill you. That was the life of the slave in your backyard.

Undoubtedly, some must have taken their chances, but most stayed under the leadership and guidance of Yagoo. As he grew older, his large beard turned gray and he began to walk with a staff, and though we don't know what religion he followed, he came to resemble a black Moses. This was how he was seen not only in the final years of his life but in his afterlife as well. When he died, he was buried on a hillock between the swamp and river, just above what is today the Millington train station in Long Hill. The burial

The Black Brook in the Great Swamp National Wildlife Refuge. This is the landscape that Yagoo and his fellow slaves were expected to turn into farmland in the late seventeenth century. *Author's collection.*

A giant freshwater clam from the Great Swamp, probably a staple for Yagoo and his people after arriving in New Jersey. They don't taste as good as they look. *Author's collection.*

ground is said to contain the remains of many of the slaves who died during that period; though no archaeological evidence of it has ever been found, it's reasonable to conclude that human remains wouldn't last long in the acidic soil, certainly not as long as the spirit of Yagoo has stayed in the swamp.

But Yagoo is not the type of ghost earthbound by the circumstances and experiences of his life, not as ghosts are generally understood. In death, Yagoo transformed into something akin to the Grandfather Spirit of the Lenapes—a spirit that is a guardian of a particular region, capable of looking into the souls of the living, knowing their motivations and helping or hindering them in their quests. He still led the spirits of the other slaves who were buried along with him but also came to interact with the living, especially those whose quests were freedom. The color of their skin didn't matter to Yagoo, for he was said to help blacks and whites alike. He guided lost Patriots and runaway slaves through the swamp, obstructed the redcoats and slave trackers who tried to follow them and even helped those who, though they didn't face the specters of bondage and tyranny, only wanted to achieve lives of their own choosing. However, physical sightings of Yagoo are very rare. As a Grandfather Spirit, his presence is more felt than seen. In the few instances where he has been seen, though, he is reported to look like he did later in his life: an old African man with white hair and a beard, wearing sackcloth robes and walking with a staff. Sometimes his hair is said to be on fire, burning but not consumed. Of course, his most powerful trait is the ability to look into men's hearts and know them perhaps better than they know themselves.

Slavery wouldn't be abolished in New Jersey until 1846, at least a century and a half after Yagoo walked the land as a mortal, and even then the break with servitude was a messy deal. Many owners transported New Jersey slaves to other states, many more tried to get the government to falsely compensate them for their financial losses and the emancipation did not extend to those slaves who came from other states. Still, with a highly active Underground Railroad, a deep-rooted abolitionist movement and an even deeper-rooted sense of right and wrong, New Jerseyians rose to the scourge that faced them and the entire nation, and Yagoo understood this. He knew that despite our bickering, squabbling and discriminating, we somehow managed to do the right thing. Thirty-three regiments of Civil War casualties and veterans buried in our cemeteries are a testament to that, as are not only those who fought in our wars but also those who stood against any injustice.

The slave in your backyard suffered a life no one could possibly envy and one no one should forget. But if you find yourself walking along the banks

The Daughter of the Swamp Oak in Basking Ridge, Bernards, is not far from Yagoo's burial site. He has been reported near this three-hundred-year-old tree just off White Bridge Road with his hair aflame. *Author's collection.*

of the Passiac River or traversing the Great Swamp and you begin to feel that someone is walking alongside you—or perhaps even catch sight of an elderly man with a staff dressed in beggar's clothing—don't be startled. Take heart in knowing that whatever cause you believe in is true because you've just won a powerful ally from the other side. That is Yagoo: African prince, colonial slave, guardian of the Great Swamp and, above all, friend to those who would live free.

4

JOHN HONEYMAN

LAMINGTON, BEDMINSTER TOWNSHIP

In Lamington Cemetery rests John Honeyman—teller of wild tales, colonist of dubious allegiance and employment and a man who may have saved the American Revolution.

I know what you're thinking: Another story of another person who saved the Revolution from failing. Go into any bookstore or browse any e-book website, and practically every history book seems subtitled "the man or woman who single-handedly altered history." The truth is that revolutions are saved at every moment of every day by every person who takes up the cause, but John Honeyman's claim to rescuing the Revolution may carry more weight than others because of when, where and to whom he told his biggest whopper. Honeyman was never shy about sharing his story of saving the Revolution—not in the eighteenth century or even now in the twenty-first.

Born in Scotland or Northern Ireland in 1729, Honeyman arrived in British North America at the age of thirty as a soldier in the British army and participated in the capture of Quebec from the French during the French and Indian War (1756–63). During the battle, the British commander, General James Wolfe, was mortally wounded, and Honeyman, who was part of Wolfe's bodyguard, claimed to have carried the general's body away from the thick of the fight, where he died without realizing the stunning victory he had achieved. Wolfe would go on to become a major hero of colonial British America. Depictions of his death were printed and widely circulated throughout the colonies. (Honeyman, so he said himself,

General Wolfe Killed at the Siege of Quebec, September 14, 1759. John Honeyman always claimed to be the redcoat cradling the general's body. *Courtesy Library of Congress.*

Griggstown, where Honeyman moved with his family in the summer of 1776. New Jersey Patriots had already been warned of his Loyalist activities as a spy. *Author's collection.*

is depicted as the redcoat cradling the dying general's body in one famous painting.) Honeyman himself, however, couldn't capitalize on this brush with glory. After the war, he settled in Boston with his wife, Mary, and worked as a weaver, butcher, cattle drover and probably anything else that could pay a shilling to feed his growing family.

With the onset of tensions between the Crown and the colonists in the 1770s, Honeyman early on became a suspicious character to the Sons of Liberty in Massachusetts for his declared loyalty to the Crown and his ability to glean information about Patriot activities. Whatever information Honeyman gave the British, if he ever gave any, didn't help them much since they were forced to evacuate Boston in early 1776. With the city firmly in Patriot control, Honeyman moved his family to Griggstown, Somerset County, later that year. His arrival in town was accompanied by a letter of introduction he probably didn't want, for the Massachusetts Committee of Safety had warned its New Jersey counterparts that they now had a notorious Tory living in their midst just as the British army was about to arrive on their doorstep in New York.

When the British invaded New Jersey in force in November 1776, Honeyman joined the British army's legion of camp followers as a cattle drover, accompanying the army on its march from Raritan Bay to the banks of the Delaware River. On Christmas Day, one of the calves he was tending broke from the herd at New Brunswick, and Honeyman left camp to search for it. What ensued was a marathon chase after the little heifer because the story then finds Honeyman captured by a Continental picket on the Pennsylvania side of the Delaware River just outside the American camp and sitting in a padlocked barn or springhouse, where he was being interrogated by none other than George Washington himself. The general, who had painstakingly spent his life cultivating the refined qualities of a Virginia plantation owner, also possessed an excellent vocabulary of salty language, which he used to rip several new ones into Honeyman during the interrogation. Washington then ordered his guards to leave him alone with Honeyman, and it was only after that, when the two men were alone, that the whole façade of this Tory sympathizer fell to the wayside.

It turned out that Honeyman had been working as a double agent for the Americans this entire time, pretending to be a Loyalist spy while gathering information on the redcoats' strength and movements throughout New Jersey. With the plans for the surprise attack on the 900 Hessians garrisoned at Trenton already underway, Honeyman gave Washington the information he desperately needed: the Hessians had relaxed their guard, making an attack on the town possible by the 2,400-man Continental army. Washington then recalled the guards, told them that Honeyman was an incorrigible Tory and ordered them to keep him padlocked until the morning when he would be hanged.

However, Honeyman's mission was only half over. Having been given the key to the padlock by Washington himself, Honeyman made his escape from the camp, crossed the Delaware, talked his way past the non-English-speaking Hessian picket at Trenton and worked himself into the late-night card game being played by Colonel Johann Rall, commander of the Hessian garrison. It was during the card game that John Honeyman told the biggest and most important lie of his life: the Americans were too weak and demoralized to launch an attack, and Rall had nothing to worry about from Washington and the ragtag rebels. For the colonel, who apparently understood English, this was exactly what he wanted to hear, despite the fact that at that very moment he was holding a note in his pocket from another visitor to the card game stating that an American attack was imminent! The note was recovered from his bloodstained coat the following morning when Rall was dead, eight hundred of his men captured, Trenton in Washington's hands and the American Revolution breathing its second wind. Honeyman had left Trenton hours earlier and returned to the British lines at New Brunswick. With the news of Trenton's fall and the ensuing bustle to launch a counterattack against the Americans, no one bothered to ask Honeyman about the calf, although he had left it tied to a tree to cover his story.

Honeyman continued to act as a double agent for the Americans during the war, although his activities concerning the attack on Trenton represent his high-water mark of espionage. He was apparently so successful in his ruse as a Tory that Washington had to write a letter of protection for his family against the Somerset County Committee of Safety, which wanted to arrest them and confiscate their property at Griggstown. The committee backed off from the Honeyman family, and John was able to elude Patriot prosecution until hostilities ceased in 1783. He even received a visit from Washington himself that year, when the general thanked him personally for his contributions to the war effort. With the truth finally able to come out, his neighbors in Griggstown realized overnight what a great Patriot this Scots-Irish immigrant had been, and Honeyman returned to his life of various employments and tale telling. Even as late as 1821, a year before his death, Honeyman was still self-promoting, claiming to be the inspiration for Camden native James Fenimore Cooper's first novel, *The Spy: A Tale of Neutral Ground.*

That was John Honeyman's story, and he stuck to it, if you believe it. The fact is that a lot of people don't believe it, and a lot do. Amateur and professional historians alike have been split over Honeyman's contributions to the Battle of Trenton for the past 237 years. Half the books and essays you'll find will state that he was invaluable to the victory. The other half won't mention him at all or will disparage his story. (Even the CIA has an essay on its website debunking Honeyman's claims.) The overall problem with John Honeyman's story has to do, ironically, with Honeyman himself. The only source for his exploits come from John and several of his descendants who became prominent in New Jersey politics and publishing and kept the story from fading into obscurity. That doesn't make Honeyman's deeds untrue, but with the lack of corroborating evidence, his claim is suspect. Were he and his family genuinely trying to keep an important contribution to history alive, or were they trying to makeover a Tory skeleton in their family closet? Unfortunately, the one man who could have settled the dispute once and for all—George Washington himself—was silent on the matter, which is not surprising.

Unraveling Washington's use of espionage during the Revolution is now entering its third century, and given the very nature of espionage, it wouldn't serve his purpose to leave a paper trail of spies and their missions for posterity or the British. Another fact is that Washington didn't necessarily need Honeyman's information. He was already committed to the attack on Trenton when Honeyman showed up in camp on Christmas and had plenty of intelligence on the Hessians from the Hunterdon and Somerset militias that had been constantly harassing the mercenaries from the moment they marched into town. Contrary to the myth, the Hessians weren't hungover when the Continentals arrived; they were exhausted. His letter of protection that Mary Honeyman waved in front of the Somerset County Committee of Safety, which no longer exists but is accepted as real, doesn't prove Washington's complicity, either; he wasn't the kind of man who took vengeance on a family for one member's actions. And as for Honeyman's claim that he was the inspiration for Cooper's novel, I have to say that, having read the book myself, *The Spy* is so full of anachronisms, romantic improbabilities and stock stereotypes that the only inspiration for it came from Cooper's own imagination; even Cooper himself admitted that he wrote the book as a bet with his sister.

Nevertheless, John Honeyman's story persists, and the debate rages on. Only now the tale of Honeyman has taken on a paranormal angle, thanks to a couple of incidents possibly linked to his spirit. In the 1980s, a photograph

Christmas Day reenactment of Washington crossing the Delaware River. Would this have been possible without Honeyman's intelligence? *Author's collection.*

was taken by an unknown person that purportedly contains Honeyman's ghost. The photo, which was published in the September/October 2005 issue of the *Black River Journal*, is of Honeyman's original tombstone in Lamington Cemetery nearly enshrouded in thick veils of mist resembling cigarette smoke. No face or figure can be discerned in the mist, yet for the last three decades, this picture has been believed to be Honeyman's spirit. However, one misty photo doesn't make a haunting, and I had never heard of anyone encountering Honeyman's ghost (or any other ghost) at the cemetery—until it happened to me.

I've been to Lamington Cemetery several times in my life, but never encountered any paranormal activity during those visits. I do believe, though, that I may have been responsible for someone else's paranormal encounter in 1993 when I fell into a grave there (not Honeyman's). The graves that border Cowperthwaite Road in the rear of the cemetery were flooded at that time, yet each was covered by a thin layer of grass, making them perfect pit traps. One tombstone caught my attention because the last name carved on it resembled the beginning of my own. I took a step closer to read it better and plunged through the skin of grass, becoming completely submerged in freezing water. I must have blacked out momentarily after falling into it because I was next aware of lying on the surface beside the grave, coughing up water, grass and—much to my horror—bone fragments.

Panicked that I'd suddenly become an accidental cannibal, I tried my best to return as much of the remains to the grave as possible, but I was covered in the tiny gray-brown shards from the top of my head to the inside of my boots, not to mention my nose, mouth and throat. When I had brushed most of the grave's occupant off me, I stumbled to my car. That was when someone emerged from the church annex adjacent to the cemetery. He took one glance at this staggering, soaking wet, corpse-covered figure emerging from the cemetery, turned around and rushed back into the annex, slamming the door behind him. Perhaps he thought that Judgment Day had arrived, but rest assured—if you ever hear a story of a wet ghost wearing a long coat stumbling from Lamington Cemetery, that was only me.

I was wet again the next time I visited the cemetery twenty years later. I didn't fall into another grave this time; it was just a stormy day. My wife and I had spent the morning in Pluckemin on an unsuccessful search for a geologic formation called the Pluckemin Stones, and we decided to drive up the highway to Lamington so I could show her Honeyman's grave. However, the weather refused to cooperate, and after ten minutes in the cemetery, Christina ran back to the car. I stayed out continuing to look for Honeyman's grave, for which, unfortunately, I had forgotten the location. With the storm growing and as I was already frustrated about not finding the grave or the Pluckemin Stones (as well as just discovering the camera I had brought with me had malfunctioned), I looked around the yard and muttered, "Where the hell are you, Honeyman?"

I suppose I said the right thing. On the south edge of the cemetery, opposite of where I was, stands a large broken oak, its trunk snapped in two about fifteen feet above the ground—it's an unmistakable landmark. Standing beside it on that rainy afternoon was a large-frame man wearing a drab, brown tricorn hat and waistcoat looking at me. He was a burly guy, someone big enough to have been a soldier or a cattle drover or a butcher. Some underbrush obscured his legs, so I couldn't see if he wore knee britches, but I could tell that he was as wet as I was. He didn't move for the several seconds I held him in sight but simply stood by the broken oak with his arms hanging by his sides until he rapidly faded from view. It would have made the perfect ghost picture—it seemed that he *wanted* me to take his picture, but there I was with a broken camera and my only other witness sitting in the car. Just like he had for the British army and the Somerset County Committee of Safety, John Honeyman slipped from my grasp.

Of course, I can't be certain it was him I saw that day in November 2013. Despite the depictions of Wolfe's death that circulated throughout

Lamington Cemetery, Bedminster, site of Honeyman's grave. Reports of his spirit have occurred here as late as 2013. *Photo courtesy of Peter and Rosemary Haynes.*

the colonies and that still exist today, it's questionable whether any of them accurately portray Honeyman. Nor was it the occupant of the grave I fell into in 1993—that was a woman's tomb. It just seems that no one else would have appeared that day I went looking for Honeyman's grave but John Honeyman himself. It would seem also that he doesn't haunt the cemetery on a continual basis, otherwise there would be more stories of people encountering him. However, given his penchant for publicity while alive, I doubt that Honeyman could pass up the opportunity for an audience, even an audience of one showing up 237 years later.

The grave marker that stands over his remains in Lamington Cemetery is a replacement erected in 2002 for the original (which is now housed inside the Presbyterian Church), and small American flags are still planted next to it as they are for all known Revolutionary War veterans. Whether Honeyman truly deserves that honor is still a matter of debate, but you can say this about such an enigmatic character: the fact that we're still debating what he may or may not have done centuries later, who he was, what he truly stood for and what he may or may not be up to now are definitely the marks of a master spy—or the marks of a master storyteller.

5

THE LIBRARY GHOST

BERNARDSVILLE BOROUGH

With one of the highest per capita income locations in the country today, Bernardsville in Somerset County can be a pretty exclusive town. Former residents like Malcolm Forbes, Jacqueline Kennedy Onassis and Charles Scribner Jr. (the publisher of F. Scott Fitzgerald, Ernest Hemingway and Thomas Wolfe) give you an idea of the kind of money you'll need to afford the place. It wasn't always like that. In its first incarnation, Bernardsville was called Vealtown because it was a colonial stockyard. It must not have smelled too good back then, but there was one thing that attracted cattle drovers and Revolutionaries and other types to Vealtown, and that was its tavern, built in 1710 along the Morristown Pike. And in that tavern was the prettiest girl in the county. Her name was Phyllis.

She was the only child of Colonel John Parker of the famous Jersey Blues, a colonial regiment in the French and Indian War (1755–63) noted for its striking blue uniforms. Colonel Parker had been wounded in the ferocious 1757 Battle of Sabbath-Day Point, which actually took place on the waters of Lake George in New York between a flotilla of canoes oared by the Native Americans and another manned by the Jersey Blues. After the war ended, Parker returned to New Jersey and raised Phyllis in the Vealtown Tavern; no mention is ever made of a Mrs. Parker, so we have to assume that he raised her alone. As her beauty grew, so did the tavern's popularity, but she wasn't the only reason behind its prosperity. Many of Colonel Parker's acquaintances from the Seven Years' War were now engaged Revolutionists and members of the radical independent state of New Jersey and the various committees emplaced for its protection that held many of their meetings at the tavern, and what better location was there for a temporary seat of government?

As New Jersey does today, it attracted a fair number of New Yorkers. However, those who came to the Vealtown Tavern in 1776 weren't tourists or migrants, but refugees from the city recently occupied by the British army. One of those fleeing the Crown was a handsome young man named Dr. Byram. The doctor soon ingratiated himself with the tavern's patrons, the innkeeper and, most especially, the innkeeper's daughter. In the midst of chaos and war, Phyllis and Dr. Byram fell deeply in love. Much to the disappointment of the single men in Somerset County, by Christmastime, they were engaged to be married.

Then, in early January 1777, a visitor came to the tavern, actually a lot of visitors—the entire Continental army. Exhausted from its victories at Trenton and Princeton, as well as its thirty-mile march to its new winter quarters at Jockey Hollow, the army marched into Vealtown. Colonel Parker and Phyllis gave them what comfort they could, as well as drams of applejack and dried beef, but Dr. Byram had retired to his room upstairs that day, complaining of an ailment. Leading up the rear of the march was the Pennsylvania Line, commanded by General Anthony Wayne, who was an old acquaintance of the colonel's from the previous war. Wayne, who was already known by his nickname "Mad" Anthony for his unorthodox tactics and temper, decided to make the Vealtown Tavern his headquarters. When he told Colonel Parker that he'd like to meet the other tavern guests, Phyllis went to Dr. Byram's room to show off her fiancé to the general. Byram, who was the only person staying in the tavern, reluctantly gave in to his beloved's pleas and accompanied her downstairs to the main room, where Colonel Parker proudly introduced his future son-in-law to General Wayne.

Wayne's reaction was anything but pleased. "Doctor my arse," he claimed. "That's Aaron Wilde, the Tory spy!"

Knowing his ruse was uncovered, for the two men knew each other by sight, Wilde—aka Dr. Byram—freely admitted that Wayne was right. However, now claiming to be Wayne's prisoner, he asked that he be given a trial to prove his guilt or innocence. It was a request that the general couldn't deny him, even though Wayne knew it could be days or weeks before a court could be convened. In the meantime, there was no jail in Vealtown to hold Wilde, the nearest one being on the Morristown Green five miles away. Instead, he was returned to his room under guard, and the door was locked behind him.

American General "Mad" Anthony Wayne (1745–1796), who moved into the Vealtown Tavern in January 1777, exposed Aaron Wilde as a spy and had him hanged. His actions would start a legendary haunting. *Courtesy Library of Congress.*

Sometime later that night, when the tavern was quiet and the exhausted guards were asleep, Aaron Wilde slipped from his room and made his escape. Since the window of his room was too small for a man to squeeze through, the door was the only way of exiting, which meant that someone must have unlocked it for him. The legend never directly accuses Phyllis of helping her lover, but it appears that she was the only one in the tavern with the motive to do it. Whether Aaron Wilde truly loved the innkeeper's daughter or was only using her to stay close to the rebels is difficult to know, but obviously Phyllis was still in love with him. After being freed, Wilde left Vealtown and made his way on the icy turnpike to Morristown, where, incredibly, he was captured again while trying to steal a horse. By this point, Wayne and the Pennsylvania Line were in pursuit and caught up with Wilde as he was being returned. Now, bound in irons and surrounded by company that was far less friendly to him than Phyllis and Colonel Parker, Aaron Wilde audaciously spoke to Wayne.

Bernardsville and U.S. Route 202 today, looking north. This is the route Aaron Wilde fled on after escaping the Vealtown Tavern. He was captured five miles away in Morristown that same night. *Author's collection.*

"I'm still entitled to my trial, general," he said.

Wayne wasn't a man for gentlemanly banter but obliged him anyway. "You're right," he answered. "You're guilty. Hang him."

Aaron Wilde was strangled by a rope draped over the nearest tree bough strong enough to hold a man's weight. After his body was lowered, Colonel Parker appeared on the scene and requested Wilde's remains. He procured a coffin, had the body put in it and returned to the tavern, where the coffin was placed on a bench table in the main room for burial the next day. Completely fatigued, everyone fell into a deep sleep, but this long winter's night still had one last act in its tragedy. Sometime before dawn, the sounds of wood being pried open were heard from the main room, followed by a blood-curdling scream. Rushing from their rooms, General Wayne, Colonel Parker and the guards found Phyllis crumpled on the floor, a fire iron by her side and Aaron Wilde's coffin lid opened. The sight of her lover's body had driven Phyllis permanently insane. All mention of her disappears from the record after that night, although it's believed that she didn't live long after it and died of a broken heart.

And this is where the story of Phyllis Parker ended for the next one hundred years. Whether the horrible events of that night replayed themselves for the future occupants of the tavern is unknown, for it wasn't until the winter of 1876–77 that the story of Phyllis's ghost made its way into public lore. On a January evening in 1877, around 6:00 p.m., a woman

had gone to the old Vealtown Tavern. The building had long since ceased serving drinks and tavern fare. By this time, it was a private residence, and she had gone there to pick up some sewing supplies from her neighbor. When she arrived, the building was dark, save a faint light emanating from the windows of the parlor, which had once been the main room of the tavern.

Before knocking on the front door, she peered through the window into the room, but what met her eyes wasn't what she expected to see. The room was no longer the elaborate Victorian parlor she knew. It was sparse, with only a long wooden table and bench in front of the fireplace. More shocking still was the simple pine coffin on top of the table and a single, lighted candle resting on its lid. The light cast itself on a young woman sitting at the bench. She had never seen the woman before, whom she described as having long, unkempt dark hair and only wearing a night shift. Thinking that someone in the house had died, she gently tapped on the windowpane to get the young woman's attention. The girl keeping vigil never responded. In fact, she appeared absolutely unaware of anything beyond the light of the candle on the coffin.

The woman finally returned home but, determined to know who had died, returned the next morning. Much to her surprise, the lady of the house greeted her and invited her into the parlor, the very room where the coffin had been last night. But no coffin greeted her eyes, no bench and no young woman—the room had been returned to its ostentatious Victorian décor. Befuddled, she began her story of what she had seen the previous night. The lady of the house was surprised by the tale, but far from incredulous. She admitted that ever since occupying the old tavern, she and her family had been plagued by many noises that petrified them every night: the sounds of many people throughout the house, the sounds of wood being torn apart and, most frightening of all, the horrific screams of a young woman. The lady of the house admitted that the house was haunted and knew exactly who was haunting it.

Not only had the story of the ghost of Phyllis Parker become public knowledge that day, but the two women's experiences would also set a precedent for how the paranormal activity of the tavern would play itself out for the next 140 years. It appears the majority of sightings of Phyllis have taken place by people who were standing outside the tavern looking in, whereas once inside, only audible phenomena could be perceived. This was confirmed by virtually every member of the Bernardsville Police Department and Bernardsville Library from the 1940s to the early 2000s, after the building became the town library; this was the period when Phyllis became known as the Library Ghost. According to one of the former police chiefs, who himself had a sighting of Phyllis while walking the beat one night, the police used to park their squad cars facing the library during their lunch breaks to try to catch sight of the pretty tavern maid through the front windows. Phyllis rarely disappointed them. However, for library employees during that time, what they encountered were strange sounds and disembodied voices, combined with the occasional misfiled book, missing object or strange behavior of electronic equipment. Phyllis didn't seem to mind people seeing her from a distance but was very hesitant to let them get closer to her.

Her reticence grew as ghost hunting became popular. The first formal investigation I heard of took place in 1974. A reporter from the local newspaper and several of her friends spent a night in the library, looking for evidence of Phyllis. Though they lacked the sophisticated detection equipment that ghost hunters can acquire today, they apparently heard many knocks and footsteps echoing through the old part of the library until midnight when a particularly loud bang from upstairs signaled an end to the investigation and the living left the library in haste. Then, in 1987, the Amazing Kreskin, world-famous professional mentalist and a New Jersey native, announced that he would hold a public séance at the library in hopes of contacting Phyllis.

I had been to the library many times since I was a child, yet nothing of the paranormal ever happened to me in or out of it. Just like the cops, I'd often peered through the windows, too. When I heard of Kreskin's intended séance, I thought that this might be my best opportunity of finally experiencing this legend. Apparently, so did several hundred other people, for on the evening of the séance, Olcott Square was choked with would-be participants. Traffic was stopped, the police were on the point of being overwhelmed and no one outside the library was allowed in; the library had already exceeded its maximum occupancy. Standing on the sidewalk just outside the library, I thought I heard some commotion coming from the inside, followed by people beginning to exit through the front door. I heard some say that the séance had been stopped. Now that there was no event to keep the throngs hanging around the library, the police hurried to break up the crowd and send us home.

After that night, Kreskin admitted that he stopped the séance because events had gone beyond his ability to control them. In the ensuing years, I have been able to see some snippets of video taken in the library from that evening. What's shown in the video is tables jumping of their own accord and the shouts and cries of the participants; this was the commotion that I'd heard from outside. Kreskin also admitted that the activity was probably not caused by any ghosts in the library, but by the energies and expectations of those in attendance, which I believed to be a reasonable explanation.

Of course, there may be another reason behind those events, which wasn't known in 1987. In fact, it wouldn't be known for nearly another twenty-five years—Phyllis isn't the only ghost to inhabit the library. In 2011, a paranormal group investigated the old building, which is now a home furnishing store, and claimed to have contacted multiple spirits in it. This included a man in eighteenth-century dress. Whether he is Aaron Wilde is unknown; no one has ever reported a male spirit in the building before this date. Another spirit is a former librarian from the 1950s–60s named Clara, who is believed to be responsible for the electronic malfunctions of telephones and computers. Then again, in 2010, the building celebrated its 300th anniversary. Never built for electricity, the tavern has gone through several major renovations in its lifetime, so it would be rash to claim that all the electrical glitches are caused by a spirit.

I thought that Kreskin was on to something about the expectations of the living entering a haunted realm. I've found that people's experience of the paranormal (or lack thereof) is dependent on what they bring to the experience themselves. After all, thousands of people, if not millions, have encountered the tavern in the last three centuries, yet only a small minority have thought something paranormal happened to them while there. But I also think that we, the living, fail to take into consideration the feelings and motivations of the dead who are still here. The horrific events of that night in 1777 literally drove Phyllis Parker insane; so long as her story remained outside the mainstream, she seemed to relive that night. Yet once the public became aware of her presence and sought her out, the haunting changed in its nature; it became more elusive or, as the video of the séance demonstrates, potentially violent. It echoes something my wife recently told me. She said, "I'm a mild-mannered person in life, so I'd be a mild-mannered ghost in death. But if someone comes into my house and provokes me, I'm going to give them a show!" I think this is especially true of a place as fickle as the old Vealtown Tavern, where the ghosts seem to have a love-hate relationship with the living.

6

THE HEADLESS HESSIAN
OF BASKING RIDGE

BASKING RIDGE, BERNARDS TOWNSHIP

O n foggy winter days along White Bridge Road in Basking Ridge, a horseman still rides. He's not a weekend equestrian renting a horse from the nearby Lord Stirling Stables, nor is he a Revolutionary War reenactor, although he does wear the high boots and midnight-blue overcoat of a Hessian cavalryman. He doesn't wear the gold-brocaded tricorn hat, either, but he can't be faulted for missing such an important part of his uniform. You see, he doesn't have a head to put the hat on.

He is the original headless horseman. In fact, he's the Headless Hessian of Basking Ridge.

How this genesis of an American legend started in Somerset County is the story of a mercenary who fought in a war he neither understood nor had a stake in. That might be harsh to say, but so was the Germany he came from in the eighteenth century. After decades of internecine fighting among Europe's royal houses, most of Germany was a fractured, ravaged and impoverished land with no opportunities for a young man except for soldiering. The horseman probably had little choice but to accept King George III's offer to help put down the idealistic rebellion of his majesty's American colonies in 1775.

At first, it must have seen like a good war to him. The rebels couldn't field an army worthy enough to stand against professional soldiers. Many Hessians couldn't even fathom why these colonists, living in such an abundant and prosperous country, would want to revolt in the first place. With each new victory, the Hessians' trepidation of meeting a new enemy

Hessian cavalry at the reenactment of the Battle of Monmouth, Manalapan, Monmouth County. This is the uniform that the Headless Hessian of Basking Ridge wears, minus the hat. *Author's collection.*

gave way to resentment, which then turned to contempt and finally to rape, plunder and burning. Just when final victory seemed imminent, however, something happened. The Americans struck back—on the battlefields, on the roads, from rooftops, from every tree and stone fence. In the dead of the late winter of 1777, there wasn't a single place in central New Jersey a Hessian cavalryman could feel completely confident in, even in places that had once seemed secure, which brings us to White Bridge Road.

Only the previous December, a unit of British cavalry dashed up White Bridge Road and captured the American general Charles Lee as he dallied with the Widow White in her Basking Ridge tavern. But those were the good days for the king's horsemen. The unit now making its way along the road was considerably smaller than Banastre Tarleton's raid—perhaps five or six horsemen compared to thirty—and far more wary. Such a reconnaissance patrol would have been unthinkable had it not been for a sudden warming of the weather, which turned the melting snow into thick veils of fog and hid their presence as they penetrated deep into American lines. They had, in fact, reached the edge of General William Alexander's (aka Lord Stirling's) estate, where a Patriot hospital and many military stores were placed. However, just

White Bridge Road in Basking Ridge, Bernards, site of the skirmish where the Hessian lost his head in 1777 and where he is still seen today. *Author's collection.*

as the fog had concealed their approach to Basking Ridge, it also hid the presence of others lurking on the edge of the Great Swamp that day.

As the horsemen reached the bridge the road took its name from, they heard the faint sounds of hooves. The fog still shrouded the unseen animals and the topography of the land scattered the sound of the pounding hooves so that it was hard to tell from where they were approaching. The Hessians stopped, each man facing a different direction, readying himself for a fight, but they were not ready enough. Out of the gloom, great steeds thundered, the American cavalrymen riding them already having their swords drawn as they came within inches of the Hessians. One Patriot slashed, sending the head of one of the mercenaries flying into the winter air. The remaining Hessians fled back from where they came, hotly pursued by the Americans. The beheaded Hessian's horse, with the body still secure in the stirrups, bolted in its own direction into the swamp. The skirmish was over as quickly as that, perhaps more quickly than it took for the Hessian to die. It's said that a suddenly decapitated head can remain alive and conscious for twenty to thirty seconds before the blood finally drains from it—it makes you wonder if the Hessian, his head coming to a rest in the roadside ditch, might have actually seen his body and horse gallop away into the fog.

Washington Irving (1783–1859), who immortalized the story of the Headless Hessian in "The Legend of Sleepy Hollow." *Courtesy Library of Congress.*

Pecked apart by birds, eaten by a bear or just washed into the swamp, the head was never recovered. Nor was the horse or body seen again, at least in a period of time when the animal could be expected to live on its own. In the decades following independence, when the armies had disbanded and peace returned and a third of all the Hessians who had tried to stop the Revolution actually became American citizens, the residents of the towns surrounding the Great Swamp began to notice a spectral white horse standing just at the edge of visibility with a rider on it dressed in the old-style uniform of a cavalryman. Seeing the rider, it didn't take them long to notice that he had no head or to realize how his spirit came to reside in the swamp, for the story of the skirmish was well known. Though the sight of the headless horseman easily struck fear into anyone unfortunate enough to see him, it appears that the ghost itself was oblivious to observers; perhaps it's a residual apparition, or perhaps because it has no head, it is unable to recognize that anyone is watching it. Either way, it was never known to attack anyone, look for its missing head or do anything except sit on the horse as a macabre reminder of the violence that had once happened there. Those other things were left for another person to bestow on him.

In the early nineteenth century, being a writer of tall tales and ghost stories wasn't a respectable profession, which was why Washington Irving staked his reputation as a biographer and travel writer. However, it was during his travels in New Jersey that he heard the story of the Hessian that ignited a spark in his brain and compelled him to write one of the first classical American ghost stories. Being a good Knickerbocker, though, he set his story in his native region of the Hudson Valley and introduced characters and attributes that had no relation to the original legend. Try as you might, you will not find people like Ichabod Crane or Brom Bones tied to the ghostly horseman, nor will you see him riding through the night with a jack-o'-lantern sitting on his shoulders in lieu of his real head. Nevertheless, the mercenary casualty of the Revolutionary War, who died nameless and unburied on a country lane in Somerset County, remains forever etched in the minds of the people he once fought against as "The Legend of Sleepy Hollow." But if you're wise to it, you'll know him by his first title: the Headless Hessian of Basking Ridge.

So should you find yourself in the swamp on a foggy day and hear the snort or stamp of a horse, take a good look around and proceed with caution. Ask yourself also if you're prepared for what you might encounter. The Headless Hessian doesn't show himself often, but if you're in the right place when he does, take a chance to see a true legend. Just don't lose your head over it.

7
KNITTING BETTY

HILLSBOROUGH TOWNSHIP

I f you've ever ventured into the Sourland Mountains on the border of Somerset and Hunterdon Counties, she has probably seen you. Perched on any of the numerous glacial boulders dotting these mountains formed during the last ice age, her life's—and afterlife's—calling has been to notice you traveling into the Sourlands. I know that she has seen me because I have seen her, and the only warning that I can give you about her is that you better have a good soul before you go into her realm or you may not come back from there.

Betty Wert was a young woman at the start of the American Revolution whose fiancé, caught up in the flush of victory at Lexington and Concord, joined the Continental army to expel the British from the American colonies. Like thousands of Patriots, he left New Jersey in 1775, went up to New England and was promptly never heard of again. Whether he ran away or died in combat or of disease, no one ever discovered, including Betty. Day after day, however, she would sit on many of the glacial rocks dotting the promontories of Neshanic and Stone Mountains in hopes of spotting her beloved's return, knitting to while away the time.

She'd end up sitting and knitting there for the next three years. Somewhere in that time she must have gotten over the loss of her fiancé, for when the theater of war shifted from New England to the Mid-Atlantic states, Betty became a spy for the Continental army. She was literally in the perfect position for the job. After the Battle of Princeton, New Brunswick became the westernmost outpost for the British army, which controlled the Raritan

The great Native American folklorist Jack Rushing sitting on a glacial rock in the Sourland Mountains, telling the story of Knitting Betty. *Author's collection.*

River all the way to Perth Amboy and across the bay to Staten Island, where General William Howe had most of his twenty thousand troops bivouacked. Washington kept them in check with his soldiers in the Watchung Mountains to the north. From the Sourlands, Betty had a front-row seat overlooking the entire Raritan Valley, where the British couldn't possibly make a move without her noticing them.

With the exception of some minor battles, such as at Bound Brook and Metuchen Courthouse, this stalemate continued until Howe bypassed New Jersey by sea to take Philadelphia in the fall of 1777, forcing Washington to make his winter encampment in the backwater of Valley Forge, Pennsylvania, which was devastating for the Continentals. The following spring, the British army, now under the command of General Henry Clinton, abandoned Philadelphia and marched across the breadth of New Jersey to return to New York. Anticipating this move, Washington tailed the British and delivered a defeat to them at Monmouth Courthouse, effectively ending all fighting in the Mid-Atlantic for the next two years. Prior to the battle, Washington used the Sourlands as a staging area for the army, and undoubtedly, some

The eighteenth-century Neshanic-Harlingen Road in the Sourland Mountains Preserve, Hillsborough. Untouched by modernization, this is one of the roads Betty Wert would have used to observe British movements during the American Revolution. *Author's collection.*

of the intelligence he gathered for the battle came from the young, pretty sentinel of the mountains. Tragically, though, Betty probably never knew how much she contributed to the American victory, for she disappeared from the Sourlands shortly before the June 28, 1778 battle.

Discovering the reason for her disappearance wasn't difficult or long in coming to the colonists. Most New Jersey Tories had been disenfranchised of their homes and property early in the war, but many remained in the state, raping, pillaging and basically murdering anyone they happened to find. There were also a number of other colonists who would have done anything for a British guinea. It's believed that Betty was captured by one of these groups and turned over to the English. At that time, even a young woman wasn't exempt from the horrors that awaited Patriot prisoners. She probably first endured the hell of a prison barge in Raritan Bay or a place like the infamous Sugar Hill Prison in Harlem before she was executed, had her head stuck on a pike in the Battery of New York City and then had her body dumped into the dunes of Sandy Hook or the mud flats of Wallabout Bay in Brooklyn. Her executioners may have been the last to see Betty alive, but they were certainly not the last to ever see her again.

In the centuries since, Betty has been reported throughout the entire Sourland region, especially near the glacial boulders and old colonial-era roads she frequented during the Revolution. However, as time and the number of sightings progressed, it seems that Betty has appeared in a variety of manifestations to the people of the Sourlands until, today, there are three distinct forms that her wraith can take: English Betty, Dutch Betty or Black Betty.

English Betty is frequently seen as a beautiful young woman peacefully knitting on the rocks along the trails and roadsides. Seemingly oblivious to observers, this manifestation of her is often reported by nonnatives to the Sourlands, who local residents generically clump under the term "English." More frightening is Dutch Betty, as seen by the descendants of the original Dutch settlers of the region, in which Betty's body, sitting on a rock, holds her decapitated head in her lap while it spins round and round and asks you to help put it back on her shoulders. The last, and most macabre, apparition is Black Betty, whose story originated among the descendants of Sourland slaves. Witnesses report a large, diaphanous cloud that is lighted from within. Inside it Betty's headless body can be seen sewing a pouch made from the flayed skins of people who commit evil in the mountains. This last form of the colonial maid is credited with a gruesome act perpetrated in the 1920s.

Throughout the area are many hamlets lost in the ravines and to time. Rock Creek in East Amwell Township is one of those places. Its only claim to fame might have been that, in 1907, a young Eugene O'Neill spent a summer there in the country home of his father, the famous Broadway actor James O'Neill, after being expelled from Princeton University. But some years later, something heinous occurred to the little town's postmaster.

The postmaster and his wife lived in a house at the crossroads of Rock Creek, near a particularly large glacial boulder. For several nights, something had been marauding the postmaster's chicken coop, slaughtering his chickens but leaving no clue to its identity. Of course, messing with a man's chickens was a major crime in those days, so the incensed postmaster tried several times to capture the pillager but never succeeded. Finally, one night, he heard a slight fluttering from the yard. Seizing his shotgun, he ran through his kitchen door, saw a dark figure by the coop, raised his gun and fired. The form instantly hit the ground. Only now fetching a lantern, the postmaster carefully walked to the shape and, in the light, saw that he had killed his wife.

Distraught, he dragged her body into the house and propped it on a chair at the kitchen table. He then went to a neighbor's house to use the phone to call the Hunterdon County sheriff. Telling the sheriff what he had done, he was told to go home and wait for the sheriff's arrival. The townspeople, awakened by the gunshot, watched the overcome postmaster return to the house and close the door behind him. Understandably, no one followed after him.

When the sheriff arrived, he knocked on the door but received no answer. Opening it, he found the postmaster's wife still propped in the chair at the kitchen table, a gaping shotgun hole in her chest. The postmaster was seated beside her, but it was no use trying to get a confession from him. His head had been completely severed from his neck, and was nowhere to be found in the house. After that, the number of Betty sightings escalated dramatically, leaving no doubt for the townspeople as to who had exacted her retribution for the crime.

In many instances, Betty has become a spirit to be feared. What follows is an account of my own experiences with her that have led me to a different conclusion. It is one of the most personal and indelible experiences I've ever had with a spirit, not because of its shock or horror, but because of her motivation behind it. Like the postmaster, I was chosen by her to have herself revealed to me, not for any crime I committed, but because I listened to her.

Here is my story of Knitting Betty.

In the mid- to late 1980s, I held a few jobs that had me traveling through the Sourlands. It was during that time that I first heard the story of Knitting Betty, but not before I had my first incident with her. On an autumn morning in 1989, I was driving along Zion Road in Hillsborough Township; I had been a staff reporter for a local newspaper for the previous several months, but that day, since I had no assignments pending, I decided to get to know the area better. Turning at the sharp corner that Zion Road makes before it leads down Neshanic Mountain, my eyes fell on a stunning brunette in a long blue dress who was sitting on a small boulder in the yard of the nearest house. At first, her head was turned slightly to the right and downward from me, her hair draped over her shoulders, and she was holding some small object in her lap that I didn't have time to recognize, for as my car came

The Raritan Valley looking east to Staten Island from the Sourlands. In the eighteenth century, the woods were cleared from the mountain slopes, providing Betty the perfect view to observe British incursions into New Jersey. *Author's collection.*

parallel to her, she looked up and we locked eyes together. Being a twenty-three-year-old man at the time, I did the most natural thing—I slammed the brakes of my car, got out and intended to introduce myself to her. However, in the two to three seconds it took me to complete those actions, she was gone. It was a large, open yard where she'd been sitting, and the full length of her skirts would have made it hard for her to dash uphill to the house. But she was nowhere to be seen. Confused and disappointed, I got back into my car and drove away.

Over the next few weeks, I went back to the corner in hopes of seeing the beautiful young woman again, but I never did. I have to state that, during my initial encounter, I didn't think for a moment that I had seen a ghost—I saw a living, breathing, if slightly eccentric, woman (after all, sitting on a rock in long skirts wasn't a common activity of Jersey girls in the 1980s) who saw me as well and then vanished. Convinced that I wouldn't see her again, I put the incident down to an opportunity missed and went on with my work and life.

The following summer, I was back at the summit of Neshanic Mountain about a hundred yards from my sighting. In the interim, I had heard the story of Knitting Betty, but that wasn't the reason for my return. Still working for the paper, I was there to interview a man who was a descendant of Mary Dubois, one of the last New Jersey slaves. Mary's story is very well documented (in fact, a predecessor of mine at the paper, Dr. Samuel Harden Stille, had written a full-length book of her life in 1877), but I never turn down a chance to learn about history. I found her great-great-grandson to be a man of wide-ranging interest and knowledge. As dark was descending and our interview concluded, I decided to ask him about his pretty neighbor at the corner, thinking there might be a last chance to meet her. After I described whom I had seen and where I had seen her, he looked at me perplexed and told me that there was no young woman matching that description living in the neighborhood. Well, I thought, so much for that.

What I didn't realize was that I had let my story out of the bag. A short while later, during one of the many township government meetings that I was required to cover and while interviewing people over a local issue, I heard an elderly woman whisper to one of her companions behind my back, "He's the one who saw Betty." Snapping round to face her, I must have startled her, because she made a hasty exit before I could ask her what she meant. That was the first time that the idea that I had seen a spirit came to me, and even then, I was far less convinced than some of Hillsborough's residents apparently were. My convincing was still a year away.

In June 1991, nearly twenty months after first seeing the pretty young woman sitting on the rock, I had gone to the newly opened Sourland Mountains Preserve on East Mountain Road. Although I knew that I was in Betty's old knitting grounds, I'd gone there to try to discover the old Neshanic-Harlingen Road, a road that predated the Revolution but was never modernized. Crossing through the Devil's Half Acre, the road itself is now the designated Blue Trail of the preserve, easily marked by two rows of tall oak trees that lead to the upper ridges of Neshanic Mountain and off park property. Now heavily wooded, both sides of the road are strewn with massive glacial rock formations, which would have made perfect observation spots when the land was cleared in the eighteenth century. (If you want an idea of the view back then, walk west for a half mile until you come to the JCP&L gas pipeline running down the mountain—the view is incredible.) Climbing the road, I was surprised how close the stones were; I was expecting them to be far off the path and lost in the brush. Now in early summer, the foliage was thick but not impenetrable, and I was able to climb and sit on a large boulder to catch my breath.

Looking around, I realized that I was the only person in the preserve that day. I started to examine some of the erratic markings on the boulder, scratchings that were made when the stones were still trapped in the ancient glacier and that, in some cases, almost resemble attempts at writing, when I heard from behind me a clear and young female voice say: "No! Here."

I turned round, and stood on the rock. No one was there. Again I distinctly heard a voice, the same woman's voice, calling, "Here." It came from farther up the road. Though I couldn't see the voice's owner, and the most appropriate reaction would have been to run in the opposite direction, I decided to follow it. Even knowing the history of violence that has been associated with Betty's spirit (and I had no doubt that it was she who called to me now), I had no ominous feelings or trepidation following the voice. This wasn't a siren leading me to doom, I realized. She wanted me to follow her.

We continued up the road. The first two times that I heard her voice I could only tell what direction the voice came from; now I could tell it was only a few feet from me, and I could sense an urgency in it, an excitement in her tone as if I was the first person in centuries who would listen to her. About another two hundred feet farther, the voice deviated from the road, leading me to another glacial boulder. Pushing past some saplings, I realized that this was a large, rounded stone, about six to seven feet high at its crest and ten to twelve feet wide, marked with the same etchings as the previous boulder but also resting on more rocks buried in the ground, which formed a small burrow. As I walked around and climbed atop the boulder, I kept hearing Betty's voice darting around it, too, repeating the same word: "Here!" From repeatedly hearing the same word, it seemed to me that she spoke it with a slight accent. I naturally presumed her accent was Dutch; after all, she was descended from the Dutch settlers to the Sourlands, and the accent was clearly from someone for whom English wasn't an original language.

After hearing her voice over twenty times, it began to slowly fade until it became inaudible. The last few times I heard it I could tell that she had stopped darting around the boulder. Although I never saw her during this entire incident, I could tell that she was standing on the opposite side of the stone from me, but her energy was fading until there was no longer any sound emanating from her. The atmosphere had lost its charge, and I felt that I was now alone. I don't know why she had led me to this particular boulder. Was it a favorite of hers or one that held more significance than the others? Was it the boulder where she was captured, the last spot where she existed as a free woman? I can't speculate beyond that but only wish that she had been able to say more to me. I realize that it must have required a lot of energy for her to accomplish what she did that day and that she chose me as the person to whom to reveal herself leaves me with a humble respect for this young Patriot.

One of Betty's rocks along the Neshanic-Harlingen Road. Betty's spirit has been seen so frequently in the Sourlands that all large glacial stones there are considered hers. *Author's collection.*

That was the last time I ever encountered Betty Wert. Though I have been back to the Sourlands numerous times in the twenty-two years since that day, I have never seen or heard from her again. I do know that when I'm back there, however, she knows I'm there, too. She knows everyone who comes there. Whether she is a gruesome or vengeful spirit for others I'll let you decide. I know who Knitting Betty is to me, and I do not fear her.

8

THE SLAVE OF MIDDLEBUSH CEMETERY

MIDDLEBUSH, FRANKLIN TOWNSHIP

S ometimes, you can stumble on stories you never knew existed and stir up ghosts that no one has ever seen. I mean that quite seriously because the one that I stirred up was a spirit who deserved to remain at rest, and he was none too pleased to be disturbed. It took me over ten years to finally understand why this event happened and longer than that to wrap my head around it. I just wish that discovering it hadn't been so disturbing to either of us.

On a cold April morning in 1994, my travels brought me to the Middlebush Cemetery on Amwell Road in Franklin Township, Somerset County. The cemetery is set far back from the road and not easily visible from it. I had to drive down what I thought was a driveway before the tombstones came into sight, and before that, I drove past a barn that could easily have dated from the eighteenth century. Once I started walking through the cemetery, I could tell that it was divided into three parts, each separated by a gravel lane: the part closest to Amwell Road contained graves from the twentieth century, the middle part held nineteenth century graves and the last part had the eighteenth century. I went straight for the colonial section, but I was stopped short by what was spread on the ground before me—dozens of toys, teddy bears and pinwheels. It seems that the cemetery association was reusing the old section for children's interments. Not colonial children, but modern ones. The sight of all those toys scattered around the children's headstones was very disturbing.

Finally walking into the colonial section didn't provide any relief, either. Most of the old red shale tombstones had been thrown onto a huge pile of dirt and cut-down rhododendron bushes, and the stones that were in place were tilted, broken and hard to read. This cemetery had the look of place that had been overgrown and reclaimed numerous times, and it looked like I had stumbled onto its latest reclamation; either that, or they were tossing aside the old graves to make way for the new ones. Toward the edge of the burial ground I saw more tombstones peeking through the brush in front of the tree line. At that time, there were only woods surrounding the back part of the cemetery.

As I walked through the graves, I saw that most of the people buried here belonged to the old Dutch families: Van Dorens, Van Lieuws, Van Veightes. The Van Dorens were the oldest and most numerous occupants who, my previous experience had taught me, were probably the original owners of this property. I even found the graves of Christian and Altje Van Doren, who, judging by their ages, were the oldest occupants of the cemetery. As I walked, however, the weather began to change. More clouds filled the sky, and the wind blew through the branches and straight into the cemetery. I thought that I would wrap up this tour and try to find a more amenable place before the weather turned bad. Walking through cemeteries and finding out about the lives of the people buried in them is most often an enlightening experience for me, but this place was depressing; I had had enough of it. Giving one last look to the cemetery, I tightened my scarf, turned up the collar of my long black overcoat and made to go back to my car. But that was when I noticed someone looking at me.

I had not seen a single person from the time I had turned into the cemetery drive—it was already a cold day and there was still some snow on the ground. However, when I turned from the graves, there was an African American man glaring at me from the tree line to the west of the cemetery. He stood at a distance of sixty to seventy feet from me, and I had a very good look at him. He was wearing a blue-checkered shirt unbuttoned midway down his chest with the sleeves rolled up past his forearms, his hair was close-cropped and his cheekbones were so high that they made his eyes look like slits. But it wasn't the fact that he seemed to be dressed for warm weather that got my attention; it was because his skin was as gray as a corpse and he stared at me with such hatred that I had to avert my eyes. In a millisecond, I knew that I was not seeing someone who was alive. When I did look back, he was no longer there, although the wind had grown fiercer and the branches of the tree where he had been standing were now flailing like they were in a hurricane.

Now would be a good time to leave, I thought. I made my way through the tombstones and into the children's part of the cemetery, but just as I got to the gravel lane, I felt two hands slam into my shoulder blades and send me crashing into the gravel.

I've had enough experience with the paranormal to know not to show fear when something malevolent occurs. Instead, I get mad, and in this instance, I was infuriated. I marched to the spot in the tree line where I had seen him, thinking that might be where he was buried. In colonial times, the poor, slaves and outcasts were often buried on the fringes of a graveyard, and sure enough, when I got to the spot, I saw several unmarked rocks in a rough line that didn't look like a natural formation. Although I couldn't see him, I felt that he was right in front of me, filled with even more anger than before. Standing on his grave, I yelled out, "You will not do that to me! I am sorry for what you had to go through, but I am not responsible for it!" All this time, the wind raged through the trees, and the sky continued to grow darker. I deliberately stayed in the cemetery for another ten to fifteen minutes, still seething; I didn't come to the cemetery for a cheap ghost thrill. I came to learn history, to honor the people from all walks of life who made it possible for us to live the lives we have today. The fact that one of them would literally throw me in the dirt was more than I could tolerate.

Well, time passed, and I went on with my explorations throughout New Jersey. Nothing of the magnitude of that event in the Middlebush Cemetery ever occurred to me again, at least in terms of its negativity. A year after this, I was recounting the story to a group of students in a folklore class when one of the students, claiming to be psychic, said that the reason the ghost was so angry at me was because I had been his owner in a past life and that I had to make amends with him. I didn't buy that claim for a moment, but I realized that there had to be some reason behind his attack. However, discovering that reason was still years away from me.

In the summer of 1996, I moved out of New Jersey to South Carolina. Before I left, though, I took one last tour of some of my favorite historical spots. Middlebush Cemetery wasn't on that list. In fact, that was the one place I had no desire to ever see again, but finding myself one day in Millstone only a mile from there, I thought that I should see it. It may sound ridiculous, but I was feeling ashamed about standing on the grave of a slave and yelling at him, even if he was the one who started the fight.

It was as if I had driven into an entirely different place from the first time. Toys still littered the children's part of the cemetery, but the pile of dirt and headstones had been removed. A new housing development had been built behind the cemetery, where there had been only woods before, but most importantly, a tall wooden fence had been constructed around the

The Van Liew Tavern in East Millstone, Franklin. Today renamed the Franklin Inn, this building once employed members of the Van Doren family, whose slave was forced to tend to smallpox victims in the family barn in 1779. *Author's collection.*

perimeter of the back of the cemetery separating it from the tree line and the slave's grave. Whereas two years earlier the cemetery had been ominous and depressing, it was now actually peaceful. Walking over to the fence, I didn't feel the least anger or rage. Perhaps that physical separation from the property was what he needed to be at peace. I still apologized for what I said to him and left the cemetery. I have never been back there, but the story still goes on.

Through Henry Charlton Beck's *The Jersey Midlands* and James Snell's *History of Hunterdon and Somerset Counties,* I had discovered that the Van Dorens were the original owners of the land that the cemetery is on, as well as the surrounding five hundred acres, and that Christian and Altje were the first settlers on it in 1723. Three of their seventeen children were also veterans of the Revolution, and because the farmstead was on one of the main roads between New Brunswick and Somerset Courthouse (Millstone), it was often frequented by American, British and Hessian soldiers, in addition to the Patriot and Tory militias roaming the back country. The Van Dorens also worked at a tavern on the east side of the Millstone River, which today is called the Franklin Inn, a condemned building that was once a used bookstore operated by the Franklin Township Library. Just as noteworthy,

Reenactors of the Queen's Rangers, a Loyalist New Jersey regiment, at the Van Liew Tavern. Such units terrorized Somerset County residents during the American Revolution and were no strangers to the tavern or the Van Doren farm located less than a mile east of here. *Author's collection.*

Statue of American general Nathaniel Greene (1742–1786), at Guilford Courthouse National Military Park, Greensboro, North Carolina. His orders to confiscate the Van Doren barn in 1779 set in motion an experience I would have with the angry spirit of a slave 215 years later. *Author's collection.*

Father Beck mentions that the Van Dorens owned three slaves during the Revolution but gives no further information about their identities.

However, the final piece of this entire experience didn't fall into place until the spring of 2005 (eleven years later), when I was in a used bookstore in the college town of Berea, Kentucky, with my wife, Christina. In that store I found a copy of General Nathaniel Greene's letters from 1778 to 1779, when he was quartermaster general of the Continental army while it was encamped at Middlebrook in Somerset County. In the book, there's correspondence between Greene and one of his deputy quartermasters, Captain John Story, centered on the Van Doren barn.

When new recruits joined the Continental army, before they could starve with Joseph Plumb Martin or get cursed out by Baron Von Steuben during basic training or face off against the Scottish Highlander Regiment, they were marched off to a secluded spot for smallpox inoculation. There, they would have an incision cut into their arms, and a doctor would smear a paste made of the scabs of smallpox victims into the cuts. From that point, nature would take its course, and if they survived, the recruits would be inoculated against one of the deadliest diseases of mankind. Captain Story approached the Van Dorens about using their barn as a smallpox hospital, an offer they first refused. The captain offered to pay them to rent the barn, but even Continental veterans wouldn't accept the paper money he had. Finally, General Greene told Story to write an IOU to the Van Dorens and confiscate the barn for smallpox inoculations, which he promptly did in late May 1779.

Obviously, if the Van Dorens didn't want to let the barn out to the Continental army, they surely would not have wanted to care for the sickened recruits once they arrived. However, they may have sent their servants to help with the care of the inoculated whether the servants themselves were immune to smallpox or not. The fact that this happened in late spring would explain why the man I saw was only wearing a shirt with his sleeves rolled up on a cold morning and why he would be upset at the sight of me wearing a white scarf like an ascot and a long dark coat and looking vaguely like a Continental officer. He might have thought that I was Captain Story returning to confiscate the barn and his services again for what had to have been the very disagreeable task of caring for the sick soldiers.

I had come to the Middlebush Cemetery looking for history. It looks like I had accidently re-created history for one unfortunate man. In the time since this incident, I have gained a tremendous knowledge and sympathy for the enslaved of New Jersey, and for my accidental role, I am sorry. I wish him peace.

9

THE SENTINEL

BASKING RIDGE, BERNARDS TOWNSHIP

L iving in such a historic area, it's not unusual to see people dressed in bygone fashions and hear them speaking with affected accents. With New Jersey's large number of historical parks and museums, reenactments and town festivals, men and women wearing colonial attire, both civilian and military, is not an uncommon sight. There are some of them you may see, though, who are not acting. I'm not writing of those who may be accused of living in the past—I'm writing of those for whom the past *is* the present.

On an autumn afternoon in 1984, patients waiting in the front room of the dentist's office on Finley Avenue in Basking Ridge were treated to the sight of a fully uniformed Continental army soldier performing his guard duty in the Presbyterian Church cemetery across the street. For over an hour, the soldier marched back and forth along the brook bordering the north side of the old graveyard, turning on his heel when he reached the end of the yard and then marching back the other way. While he marched, he seemed unaware of the twentieth-century traffic whizzing along the road, as well as the dentist's patients in the waiting room who were regarding him with great interest since there were no events being held at the church or in town that would call for a reenactor that day. In addition to being oblivious to the cars and patients, the soldier was also unaware of the more modern tombstones that were now placed in that area of the churchyard because he walked right through them on his march.

What those patients had seen that day was the most famous appearance of one of the wraiths collectively known as the Sentinel. Throughout Morris,

The Presbyterian Church and its five-hundred-year-old oak tree in the center of Basking Ridge, Bernards, site of the most famous Sentinel sighting. *Author's collection.*

Actual location of the Basking Ridge Sentinel sighting at the rear of the Presbyterian churchyard. *Author's collection.*

Somerset and Union Counties, these ghostly sentries have been seen on duty nearly a quarter millennium after the Revolution ended. Many of the locales they have been spotted in haven't been as prominent as the center of a town like Basking Ridge but rather remote—mostly in woods or near brooks, places not generally traveled to by the living. This isn't unusual when you take into consideration the nature of the Continental army encampments in New Jersey. During four of the seven winters of the Revolutionary War, the American army had turned central New Jersey into a widespread base, with posts, forts, signal towers, artillery parks and pickets from Bound Brook to Pluckemin to Morristown to Summit, an area encompassing about two hundred square miles. The sites that the Sentinel has been seen—remote as they may seem in the twenty-first century—in all likelihood held some military significance in the 1700s.

The general description of the Sentinel doesn't change with the locations where he has been seen: a Continental soldier performing picket duty. It does appear that there is more than just one individual soldier who is called the Sentinel and that some are residual energies whereas others are intelligent entities. One of those entities harkens back to the Basking Ridge sighting, but this particular sentry is not merely repeating an action oblivious to the modern changes around him. He's actually still on duty, and he will challenge you if you come too close.

Sighted along Green River Road in the Great Swamp, as well as numerous places throughout the Watchung Mountains and Somerset Hills, an African American soldier still guards the twenty-four known locations where his comrades are buried. These locations are not formal cemeteries, and the bodies buried in them are not of veterans; these are the unmarked, hastily arranged interments of the boys and men of the Continental army who died of disease, wounds and hunger while the war was still happening. This sentinel is said to be a tall, imposing figure, immaculately dressed, who performs his maneuvers with perfect precision, just as his descendants do today at the Tomb of the Unknown Soldier in Arlington National Cemetery, except that he has no eyes in his sockets. The fact that he is eyeless doesn't prevent him from noticing intruders, for it is said he will stop marching and point his bayonet-tipped musket at people who approach the cemeteries. He doesn't speak, and what he would do if a person kept approaching isn't known because no one has stayed around long enough to find out.

I've heard it said that he's still on duty under the direct orders of George Washington himself. In 1775, when Washington arrived in Cambridge, Massachusetts, to take control of the Continental army besieging Boston,

Continental army reenactors in Delaware regimental uniforms at the Battle of Guilford Courthouse, Greensboro, North Carolina. The African American Sentinel reported in Somerset County is said to wear a uniform similar to these. *Author's collection.*

the Virginian was uncomfortable with the sight of black and white soldiers living and working together and tried to segregate them. However, because of recruitment problems and resistance from the New England regiments, he abandoned that plan and allowed the African Americans (many of whom were freeborn men) to serve in the full capacity of soldiers. This policy continued as the theater of war shifted to the middle states, where many of the African American recruits were the slaves of owners who substituted them for their own military duties. Because he witnessed firsthand that they served with as much bravery and honor as their white counterparts, Washington formed an all-black unit of soldiers, whose duty was to guard the graveyards of fallen soldiers, a very high military distinction for any soldier. It's possible that seeing these African American men, who composed between 20 to 25 percent of the Continental army, defend the memory of their fallen comrades may have contributed to Washington's changing views about African Americans. Washington came to oppose their enslavement but, like most of the founding fathers, was unable to make the step for their full emancipation and citizenship. Unfortunately, this brief moment of equality and acknowledgement wouldn't last. After the Revolution ended, the armed forces of the United States were segregated and would remain so until 1950.

The last of the Sentinels is, I believe, not a sentinel at all, but this ghost has somehow become included among the soldiers who still perform their duties. Seen in the woods of Bernardsville and Bedminster, Somerset County, this spirit is a young man who wears the billowy white shirt and knee britches commonly worn in the eighteenth and early nineteenth centuries, although he wears nothing else that would distinguish him as a soldier. Bleeding heavily from his shoulder or arm, he stumbles in great pain through the woods, unheeding of people who see or try to help him. Who he is and how he received his injury is unknown, and he always seems to disappear before his journey is resolved or when people get too close to him. It's sad to write, but it seems that the last moments of this unknown young man's life will forever play out in the woods for those who journey into them.

These are the Sentinels of New Jersey. If you see one, remember that they are not there to scare you. They are there to remind you of their stories full of dedication, honor and tragedy, and like those of all old soldiers, their sacrifices will never fade away.

10

THE GRAVES
IN THE CANAL

SOUTH BOUND BROOK BOROUGH

No matter what the season, a walk along the tow paths of the Delaware & Raritan Canal is a transforming experience. Coursing sixty miles through Hunterdon, Mercer and Somerset Counties, the D&R (as it's also known) is bucolic New Jersey at its best, offering the traveler tranquil waters, shady mulberry trees and up-close encounters with native wildlife along every mile—completely obscuring the toil, turmoil and death it exacted in its construction. For those aware of the tragedy of the canal's beginnings, it is surprising to learn that there is little paranormal activity associated with it today, except for one tiny portion of the canal in the little borough of South Bound Brook, Somerset County. Before we get to that, however, let me tell you the story of the Delaware & Raritan Canal.

As far back as 1671, people had wanted to build a safe, traversable waterway across the peninsula of New Jersey. To the early colonists and to those living at the start of the Industrial Revolution, the reasons for a canal were obvious: the time and danger involved in sailing the Jersey coast and the unpredictability of the inland rivers made waterborne transportation a treacherous and costly endeavor. The lack of a water route was literally impeding the growth and progress of the nation's cities, especially that of New York City, which was rapidly turning into the trade and immigration hub of the United States. With the discovery of the vast anthracite coal fields and iron ore deposits in Pennsylvania in the early nineteenth century, New York could have been on the verge of a massive explosion of prosperity except for one obstacle: New Jersey's lack of a fully navigable river to bring that coal and iron to the city.

An attempt to remedy that was made in 1827 with the construction of the Morris Canal. However, the canal stopped seven miles short of breaching the Delaware River, making it commercially unviable. Five years later, though, U.S commodore Robert Stockton of Princeton, grandson of Declaration of Independence signer Richard Stockton and renown poet Anne Boudinot, was able to collect $2 million in public bonds and private investments to start work on the long-planned but always delayed canal connecting the Delaware and Raritan Rivers. But even by then, canals were already passing their heyday, and Stockton couldn't have garnered his investment without agreeing to build the new, cutting-edge technology of his time alongside the canal—a railroad. For that, he enlisted John and Robert Stevens of Hoboken, steam power engineers who had been locked out of the steamboat trade by Robert Fulton's monopoly of it along the Hudson River. Stockton also hired his friend Canvass White, engineer of the Erie Canal who had brought from England the formula for waterproof cement—a formula first perfected by the Romans but lost until its rediscovery in the late eighteenth century—essential to the canal's success.

By a great stroke of luck for Stockton, he had a ready workforce available to start construction on the canal. Congress had recently decided to mothball the entire U.S. Navy that year, putting nearly three thousand shipyard workers of the Brooklyn Navy Yards out of work. Most of these workers were Irish immigrants who would have found it difficult gaining new employment in the era of "No Irish Need Apply," so the commodore invited them to work on the canal and railroad in New Jersey. By August 1832, thousands of workers were in place from Lambertville to Princeton to New Brunswick, ready to start the project. However, there was also another new arrival to America that had joined them and that almost stopped the project as soon as it had begun—the Asiatic cholera.

It was a global pandemic six years in coming to New Jersey. First identified in India in 1826, cholera made its way along the global trade routes, through the Middle East, along the African coast, into the Mediterranean and finally striking England and North America simultaneously that summer. The first cases of cholera appeared in Kingston along the Millstone River and quickly spread through all the canal camps. Because of its virulence, it spread fear and panic through the entire state—the bacteria moved so quickly a person could go to bed that night and be dead by morning, having literally defecated all the water from his organs. Not many survived twenty-four hours after contracting the bacteria, and the treatment for it at the time—drinking a solution of mercury—was practically as dangerous as the disease itself. Construction was halted. The campus of Princeton College became a field hospital for the Irish.

The Delaware & Raritan Canal lock at South Bound Brook, constructed in 1832. Sightings of a Chinese funeral procession have been reported along the adjacent tow path here. *Author's collection.*

Fields and woods became unmarked cemeteries for the dead. Death stalked New Jersey with a vengeance not seen since the Revolution.

Stockton, the Stevenses, the Medical Board of New Jersey and many local doctors attempted to stem the spread of the disease. Some of their efforts were successful, but eventually the cholera ran its course. It had largely disappeared by the autumn. Work resumed on the canal and railroad, which was finally completed two years later. From its opening day, coal flowed to New York City. In twenty years, the city would begin to look like the megalopolis we recognize today. Stockton remained as president of the D&R until his death in 1869, occasionally making career detours like conquering California during the Mexican-American War (1846–48), commanding the first steam-powered ship of the U.S. Navy (the USS *Princeton*) and serving as U.S senator until the start of the Civil War. The Stevens brothers would go on to build and own the Camden & Amboy Railroad, the forerunner of NJ Transit, and their estate in Hoboken would become the Stevens Institute of Technology, one of the nation's premier engineering schools. Canvass White died weeks after the canal's opening in 1834 from tuberculosis and a body weakened from a combat wound received in the War of 1812. He's buried

The graves of the first Irish canal workers who died of the cholera outbreak in 1832 in Griggstown. These men were lucky to be interred properly. Later victims were hastily buried near where they died. *Author's collection.*

in Princeton Cemetery, not far from Stockton and his wife or from the canal that exacted such a heavy cost for the price of progress.

The precise number of deaths that resulted from building the D&R—whether from cholera or work-related accidents—is unknown, but that number easily reaches into the hundreds. However, there are only eight known graves of Irish who died from that period, located and commemorated in Griggstown with a plaque and eight small Irish and American flags. Paranormally speaking, you'd think the entire sixty miles of the canal would be chock-full of restless Irish spirits, but there are no stories of Irish ghosts wandering the paths and fields along the waterway. In fact, there are almost no ghost stories associated with the building of the D&R, except for one. One group has left its mark on the canal, both literally and otherworldly, and if you're willing to venture there, you might be able to find it.

After Stockton's death, the D&R fell on hard times. The railroad became the prime transporter of coal and people across New Jersey. To make the canal competitive, the new owners decided to widen the canal to increase its traffic, but labor was coming up short for the project. To that end, they

Amid this overgrowth at the D&R in South Bound Brook is a Chinese tomb marker. The area has been renovated since this image was taken in 1994. *Author's collection.*

hired hundreds of itinerant Chinese laborers, the first time people from that part of the world entered New Jersey in significant numbers. However, their presence was all but concealed; due to the discriminatory laws and attitudes toward Asians in the nineteenth century, they were isolated from the nearby towns, paid exceptionally low wages (if at all) and refused burial for their dead in any established cemetery. When one of their friends and co-workers died, the Chinese literally buried the body into the earthen walls of the canal. They were, however, allowed to erect tombstones to their fallen friends, traditional-style pillars inscribed with Chinese writing that are still visible today. These are located about two hundred yards east of the lock in South Bound Brook. When I first saw them in 1992, that part of the canal had not been kept up. Back then, it was choked with lilies, the tow path was uneven and I had to pass the ruins of a train trellis and a hill of asbestos before looking down the shrub-filled embankment and seeing the square tops of the tombstones poking from the water. Today, that portion of the D&R has been restored, and there is a condominium development directly across the canal from the graves. Depending on the level of the water, you'll

Water lilies growing along the canal banks are said to mark the sites of Chinese laborer interments. *Author's collection.*

see between five and eight black stones, and if the water level is exceptionally low, you might be able to make out the calligraphy carved into them over a century ago.

The tombstones are not the only reminder of these souls who passed here, for it's said that on rainy days, a funeral procession can be seen slowly making its way along the tow path toward the graves. Witnesses have reported a horse-drawn cart carrying a body wrapped in linen proceeding along the path, followed by a procession of people carrying lanterns who are all dressed in white—the color of mourning in Chinese culture. This is the last reminder of these people who came from halfway across the planet to New Jersey, toiled on this small part of a canal that helped turned a wilderness nation into a global superpower and died nearly forgotten by those who followed.

If you're ever at the D&R, whether walking its paths or canoeing its waters, take a moment to remember those forgotten men, both Irish and Chinese, who gave so much for this land and you. They just might acknowledge your appreciation by showing themselves to you or tossing a lump of coal in your direction. Don't be offended if they do—it was the reason they went there in the first place.

PART II
MONSTERS

11
THE GREAT SWAMP DEVIL

GREAT SWAMP NATIONAL WILDLIFE REFUGE, SOMERSET COUNTY

Anybody who knows anything about New Jersey knows about the Jersey Devil—the cursed thirteenth child of Captain and Mrs. Leeds who was born on a stormy night in 1735 at Leeds Point, Atlantic County; transformed from a human infant into a six-foot-tall winged demon with cloven hooves; and now resides deep in the Pine Barrens of South Jersey. But did you know that he has a northern cousin who calls the Great Swamp National Wildlife Refuge of Somerset and Morris Counties home? He's a little younger than his more famous relative and bears a striking family resemblance, too. He's also more publicity shy than the Jersey Devil, but that doesn't mean he won't make his presence known when the mood or necessity strikes him. And when it does, lock your doors, huddle in the safest corner of your house and don't stir until you no longer hear the heavy hoof beats racing across your rooftop. The Great Swamp Devil is on the prowl, and he's not a neighbor most want to make friends with.

There is no genesis story for the Great Swamp Devil. He's not connected to any colonial family, at least as far as we know, and like his southern counterpart, trying to find his hoof prints in Native American lore is elusive due to the vast number of mind-bending creatures that inhabit it. What we do know is that he was first spotted in the Great Swamp on a night in 1745 by a Dutch parson who was returning home after visiting an ailing parishioner. The parson reported that as he drove his wagon along White Bridge Road toward Basking Ridge, his horse became startled and hard to control. As he struggled to get the horse moving again, he saw two bright, glowing green

Composite sketch of the Great Swamp Devil of Somerset County, based on several sightings of the creature in the 1980s. *Author's collection.*

eyes staring at him through the brush. At first the eyes were all that he could see, but as the creature shifted, the parson was stunned to see that it was not only as tall as a man but also covered in hair and seemed to have some kind of appendages on its back. Being a man of religion, he instantly suspected that this was no usual swamp animal but rather something from the depths of hell. The creature then obliged his suspicion when the appendages on its back sprung wide to reveal huge, leathery wings that it began to flap. With thunderous claps, it started to rise slowly off the ground and then shot through the trees at an incredible speed, leaving the parson alone on the road with his frightened horse and a new, horrifying legend.

In the years after the parson's sighting, the devil was seen from time to time throughout the swamp, flying low over the rivers and streams and snatching fish in midflight; heard scrambling across rooftops and barns in the night; or sometimes making long, mournful howls that echoed for a great distance. Though no one could claim that he caused any harm to them or their property, just the thought of sharing the same realm with such a creature filled the colonists with fear—that is, except for one colonist. To say that what he had planned for the devil was brave or foolhardy or just outright insane is a matter of debate. Whatever your opinion of his actions is, his confrontation with the Great Swamp Devil permanently linked the two together in folklore and stamped the legend of the devil forever on the swamp.

William Alexander was the heir of a powerful and wealthy New York family in the decades before the Revolution. That wealth came largely from vast land holdings in New York and New Jersey, of which the Great Swamp was one and where William chose to build his own estate. Before he built his great manor house on the bluff between Basking Ridge and the Passiac River, however, he tried to get himself crowned king of Scotland. In 1745, the same year that the devil made itself known to the parson, Bonnie Prince Charlie's rebellion erupted in Scotland and very nearly succeeded in wresting the country free of England's centuries-long domination of it. Though the British quickly regained their control over Scotland, Parliament toyed with the idea of reestablishing the Scottish monarchy as a way of controlling its unruly subjects, an idea on which Alexander enthusiastically seized. With no delay, he claimed for himself the title of Lord Stirling, sailed to England and petitioned Parliament to become its puppet king. Though Alexander did have royal blood in him, Parliament eventually rejected the entire plan, and Alexander—that is, Lord Stirling—returned to New Jersey, having gained nothing from the government.

He didn't return empty-handed, however, for he had gained the respect of thousands of angry Scots refugees who had fled to Ireland after the rebellion's failure and who followed him to America. Once back in Basking Ridge, he continued his royal airs, riding about the colony in a coach brandished with the Alexander coat of arms, dressing his servants in elaborate costumes befitting of an aristocrat's attendants and insisting that he be addressed as "Lord Stirling" rather than "Mr. Alexander." Since he was still a wealthy and well-connected man and his self-adopted royal standing didn't extend to oppressing his neighbors, his eccentricities were indulged by his fellow colonists. However, there was still a pressing problem he had to resolve regarding his estate. Like many gentry colonists, the bulk of his wealth lay in land. Unlike many of them, though, he also owned a rather large amount of cold, hard cash—and in the eighteenth century, that meant gold and silver. He had intended to place his treasure in a tunnel constructed between his manor house and the river, but he wasn't completely assured of its safety there. After all, he wasn't always at the estate to keep an eye on it, and the tunnel was the worst kept secret in the colony. He needed something else to secure his treasure, and who better to guard an eccentric lord's wealth, he thought, than the devil himself?

What ensued was probably the most bizarre and dangerous hunt in New Jersey history. Hundreds of men, dogs and horses fanned out and combed through the Great Swamp in search of the devil. They actually succeeded in flushing him out, chasing him through the forests and marshes until he was somehow lassoed around the Great Swamp Oak near Lord Stirling's estate, a then five-hundred-year-old oak tree that still stands today. You can still see the faint rope marks and bullet holes in its trunk and get an idea of the reeling sight those colonists saw the day they snared the beast against it: dozens of men fearfully holding the ropes and chains tied round the creature, dogs barking insanely and snapping at its limbs and wings, horses throwing their riders, more men firing their muskets and shotguns into it, the bullets simply evaporating into its body with no visible effect and, all the while, that incredible beast from another realm snarling, slashing and letting out ungodly howls that pierced into their very souls. Eventually they corralled the devil into the river entrance of Lord Stirling's tunnel, sealing him behind a heavy iron gate. They then bricked-up the entrance to the tunnel three feet thick and buried it in tons of earth. The lord's treasure was safe, they thought, now and forever.

Well, not really. A couple weeks later, that crafty devil was once again seen flying and hopping throughout the swamp, doing his devilish things of fishing and showing himself to people. How he got out of the tunnel is unknown, but no one, including Lord Stirling, wanted to go through the ordeal of putting him back in there. Alexander seemed satisfied that the legend of the Great Swamp Devil in his tunnel was enough to safeguard his money. Besides, history would soon distract his attention away from his treasure. When the American Revolution broke out, he became a Patriot general and served with distinction for the cause of independence. Though not of the caliber of generals like Nathaniel Greene, Anthony Wayne or Benedict Arnold, Lord Stirling proved to be one of Washington's more competent generals, covering the retreat of the American army at Gowanus Creek in Brooklyn during the disastrous Battle of Long Island in 1776, where he was captured by the British but later paroled. After briefly serving as quartermaster general of the Continental army, he led a courageous counterattack at Metuchen Courthouse in the spring of 1777, which helped drive the British out of New Jersey for the remainder of the year. He died in Albany, New York, in 1783, at the age of fifty-seven, having earned, despite his eccentricities, the respect of his countrymen—and yes, even George Washington called him Lord Stirling. His manor house in Basking Ridge burned to the ground about twenty years later, taking with it the location of its tunnel and the treasure within, but not the story of the Great Swamp Devil. He had other mischief to make, and other people to torment.

In the extreme northwest corner of Somerset County, miles from the swamp, sits the little settlement of Pottersville, Bedminster Township. Time moves slower there, and development has yet to catch the little hamlet like it has the rest of the county. The old houses sit a little dilapidated, and the lanes that lead off deep into the forests and abandoned fields of Hunterdon County have not been widened. It was here on a bitterly cold winter's night in 1888 that a local resident and his family had a terrifying encounter with the devil.

Henry Able, his wife and children were returning home from church services in their wagon when their horse reared and stopped in the middle of the stone bridge that crosses the Lamington River in the middle of town. The horse couldn't be blamed for being spooked, for standing in front of it was a beast that defied all logic. Standing six feet tall, with a wingspan twice that length, stood a creature covered in hair with glowing green eyes in its wolf-shaped head, huge clawed hands and heavy cloven hooves. It let out a sound unlike any animal ever heard, a *wree*-like wail that went straight into the bones of the Able family. The devil then shot into the air, and flew not only in circles just inches above the wagon and the horrified family but also under and over the bridge. Henry claimed that the beast terrified them for nearly an hour in this manner, while his horse was unable to move and no neighbor or traveler happening on the scene to help—as if anyone could have possibly helped them in that situation. All the frightened family could do was huddle in the wagon bed while Henry furiously slapped the reins on the horse's rump to get it to move, but the horse seemed to be in a trance and would not budge. Finally, the devil flew in a wide loop above the bridge, and the horse seemed to come back to life and bolted down the lane, taking the wagon and the Able family with it. Once away from the bridge, the Ables no longer saw the creature and returned home, but the devil was apparently not done with them. Henry claimed that, in a dream he had later that night, the Great Swamp Devil appeared and spoke to him, which is an amazing feat; not even the Jersey Devil has been known to utter language! It was only one sentence that the devil spoke to Henry, but the message was unmistakable: "Leave New Jersey, or you will be doomed."

What the Great Swamp Devil had against him is unknown. Henry was a very average man for his time, with no known vices or misdeeds to his name. However, he didn't need to be told twice to heed the creature's dream message, and the next day, he packed up his family and their belongings and abandoned their home and the state, never to return. In fact, he left in such haste that he didn't pay the debts he left behind, but money is a small matter to consider when a devil tells you to get out.

This dramatic encounter with the Great Swamp Devil became a tale told far and wide in New Jersey and may have actually sparked a rivalry with his southern cousin. Thirty-one years later, starting on January 12, 1909, and culminating seven nights later, was the "Famous Week" of Jersey Devil sightings. For the entire week, a bizarre creature was spotted in the yards and on the streets of cities and towns throughout Burlington, Middlesex, Mercer and Somerset Counties and even into Philadelphia and Pennsylvania. In their respective neighborhoods, policemen, trolley car operators, town councilmen and other respectable witnesses all reported seeing a bizarre, winged creature, racing across rooftops, hitching rides on trolley cars and fighting off neighborhood dogs. The creature moved with incredible speed, being seen in one town and then spotted only minutes later in another dozens of miles away. Stories of these sightings were even reported in the *New York Times* and *Philadelphia Inquirer*, transforming the devil of New Jersey from a local legend into a national phenomenon. The story is fully documented in McCloy and Miller's classic *The Jersey Devil*, but I've always wondered if some of the northerly sightings of the devil during that week over a century ago might have actually been of the Great Swamp Devil rather than his Pine Barrens relative. Sightings of the beast were recorded in Somerville, Somerset County, and New Brunswick, Middlesex County, that week, both of which are much closer to the Great Swamp than the Pine Barrens and the majority of the other encounters. Perhaps the devil cousins were trying to outdo each other in how many people they could frighten. I have to concede that the Jersey Devil won that particular contest, becoming an American monster decades before Bigfoot, Champ and Mothman reached that status, but that didn't discourage our friend from the swamp. He still had a few tricks in his wings.

The Great Depression struck New Jersey just as hard as the rest of the country, causing mass migrations of people from one part of the nation to another in search of better lives. While many midwesterners fled to California to escape the environmental disaster of the Dust Bowl, many also fled eastward. In the early 1930s, two such young men named Bill and

Bob found themselves working in the Great Swamp with the Works Progress Administration (WPA), part of President Franklin Delano Roosevelt's New Deal plan designed to alleviate the economic stress of the Depression. Their job was to dig ditches to drain the marshes on the western side of the swamp, near the Passiac River and the long-overgrown estate of Lord Stirling. Neither man knew the history or folklore of the area when they started the project in midsummer, which had to have been a difficult but appreciated task since they were working when millions weren't. As their shovels struck the ground, the earth beneath gave way, revealing a deep hole. Instantly, though, both men saw the red bricks surrounding the hole and realized that they must have stumbled on a man-made structure beneath the surface. Though they couldn't see into the cavern, both Bill and Bob were curious and adventurous enough to want to explore it.

When the day's work was done, they returned to the site of the opening again with their shovels, along with a couple of lanterns and some rope. Widening the hole enough to fit through, Bob was lowered into it while Bill anchored him. It turned out that the hole was only six or seven feet deep, and when Bob touched the bottom, his feet landed on a brick floor instead of dirt. Though it was nearly pitch-dark, he could tell that he was standing in a long tunnel—the first man to do so in nearly 170 years, for they had in fact rediscovered Lord Stirling's tunnel.

Bill handed him a lantern, but no sooner had Bob gotten it in his hands and started to adjust its light then he sensed a stirring inside the tunnel with him. In an interview conducted with the two men in the 1980s, Bob claimed that he was only able to perceive a faint glimmer of gold light emanating around him in the tunnel before he caught sight of two glowing green lights staring at him from the darkness that started to move toward him. Not waiting to see what was behind those lights or bothering to grab a few coins from Lord Stirling's treasure, Bob scrambled out of the hole, and both men ran for their lives. Neither ever attempted to return to the tunnel or to the thing inside it again.

Bill and Bob may have been the last people to see the tunnel to date, but they certainly aren't the last to see the devil that had been imprisoned there, albeit briefly, in 1765. For the last eighty years, the Great Swamp Devil has still been seen prowling the swamp, but he seems to have undergone an attitude change toward his human neighbors. No longer dedicated to frightening or tormenting us, he seems to have a cautious interest in our activities. Joggers and hikers who use the old trails and roads in the swamp often find themselves with an unexpected partner following them just out of

The Black Brook of the Great Swamp National Wildlife Refuge, where the devil was first seen in 1745. This is also one of the devil's favorite fishing spots. *Author's collection.*

sight in the brush, catching only the briefest glimpses of something huge or hearing a weird chattering noise accompanying them on their treks. Given the devil's purported size and speed, a human would be a quick catch if it were actually hunting them, but this doesn't appear to be its objective. Nevertheless, it's probable that some unofficial speed records have been broken by people who thought that the swamp would be a good place to jog. In fact, his new hobby has caused the annual 5K race there to be named the Great Swamp Devil Run.

Sightings of the devil escalate during particularly harsh winters, when the snow is deep and food scarce. This is when he ventures from the deepest recesses of the swamp and into the residential areas surrounding it. Unlike jogging with the runners in summer, though, he prefers a different mode of travel in winter. From rooftop to rooftop he flies, leaving his hoof prints in the snow like old-fashioned calling cards. His prints have been photographed and published a number of times in newspapers and magazines, especially in the winters of 1993, 1994 and 2003, all of which were harsher than average. In all those instances, wildlife experts and police have been stumped by the evidence left behind. The tracks don't match known animals, and the sheer size of them would out rule local wildlife, unless a two-hundred-pound goat has learned to hop from one house to another a hundred yards away. It's not bad for a creature that's almost 270 years old.

What the future holds for the Great Swamp Devil in his next quarter-millennium no one can say. So far, he's made it through colonization, industrialization and suburbanization. He's been chased, captured, shot, imprisoned and given up to myth. With the wings of a bat, the head of a wolf, the trunk of a man, the claws of a panther and the legs and hooves of a goat, he certainly doesn't fit into biology as we know it. He's a supernatural creature, what the ancient Greeks called a chimera, a creature composed of different animal parts that also possessed a mysterious purpose to those it encountered. His presence and purpose may remain a mystery to us. Perhaps he's there to remind us that there is more to existence than we can realize, that there are indeed monsters in our woods as well as our psyches. But if you ever hear his mournful wails echo from the swamp forests or the thunderous billowing of huge wings starting to take flight just outside your window, you will know without doubt that the Great Swamp Devil exists. Have a little sympathy for him, though. After all, it can't be easy being a monster, especially a devil.

12

SERPENTS AND PANTHERS

BRIDGEWATER, BRANCHBURG AND HILLSBOROUGH TOWNSHIPS

U nlike many states, New Jersey is fairly free of snakes and panthers. The biggest snake species you might encounter is the harmless garter snake, which you'd probably not know was even there until you ran over it with your lawnmower. And chances are that you'll never see a wild bobcat in your entire life (although they are here), much less a cougar. That wasn't always the situation, however. In its early incarnation as the colonial frontier, the Jerseys were as full of cottonmouths, copperheads, rattlers and panthers as the rest of North America. But we don't have a Jersey St. Patrick to thank for eradicating the snakes, nor were all the big cats stuffed and mounted in museums by big-game hunters. That took a lot of hard work by the early colonists. In fact, half the history of seventeenth-century New Jersey could be summed up in seven words: chopping trees, killing snakes and shooting panthers. Although colonists succeeded in getting rid of the dangerous predatory species, they didn't eliminate the weirder ones.

These are very strange and rarely seen creatures, but if you believe the old tales, you might be able to find some of them. They're not entirely biological animals, brought into existence by millions of years of evolution and mutation like you, me and all other life around us. These creatures, like the dragons of the Old World, are preternatural beings, forged from the early chaos of creation by whatever forces saw fit to make them. As such, they are beings in possession of the dualistic elements of life—chaos and order, despair and wisdom, deprivation and generosity. They cannot be approached lightly, nor with malevolence or greed, because you in no way are stronger, smarter or wiser than they are. Perhaps the wisest move would be not to seek them out at all, but should you find yourself in their realms, here is what you might encounter.

The Watchung Mountain Range is the first significant high terrain of the Appalachian Mountains in central New Jersey. Though technically not mountains (their elevations don't exceed one thousand feet above sea level), they have been the highest vistas above the valleys of southern New Jersey for the last 65 million years. The range is also the home of the Giant Worm, a creature said to be one hundred feet in length, ten feet wide with two glowing yellow eyes as large as headlamps. Since worms don't have eyes, that last detail would seem to make it more serpentine, but to the Lenapes who first saw it, it resembled a worm more than a serpent. This creature is said to remain underground most of the time, traveling through caves believed to riddle the whole mountain range from Paterson to Pluckemin, but occasionally emerges onto the surface at night, when its eyes make it highly visible through the forests. One of these entrances was (or still is) believed to be on the northern slope of the mountain between Newman's Lane and Crim Road in the Martinsville section of Bridgewater Township on property that is today Washington Valley Park. It was in this area in the latter half of the nineteenth century that residents reported seeing two large balls of yellow light, spaced apart like eyes, moving through the forests—remember, this was in the time before motorized vehicles, and the witnesses would not have been fooled by a couple of lanterns swinging from a wagon.

According to the Lenapes, the Giant Worm is the guardian of the mountain range, protecting some kind of resource deep within it. What that resource could be is unknown. Over the last two centuries, the Watchung Mountains have yielded only low-grade copper and iron; today, the largest resource mined from them is gravel. But the Lenapes didn't value raw ores for industrial purposes like Westerners, and apparently neither does the Giant Worm, so whatever it's protecting is something beyond our current understanding of the mountains. Then again, only thirty-five miles northwest of Martinsville is the Sterling Mine and Museum in Ogdensburg Township, Sussex County, a site that has yielded some of the most unique gemstones on the planet, which the Lenapes would have valued. Perhaps a similar discovery waits in the Watchung Mountains, guarded by the Giant Worm.

For the past decade, sightings of panthers have been on the rise. Reports of big cats have occurred in nearly all corners of the state, from the heavily suburbanized Passaic County township of Hawthorne to the rural Delaware River town of Lopatcong in Warren County and the Pine Barren city of

A rock carving discovered by the author at Chimney Rock, Bridgewater, in 1996. Whether it's Lenape or colonial in origin is uncertain, but it was found in an area alleged to be inhabited by the Giant Worm. *Author's collection.*

Vineland in Cumberland County, as well as along the northern border of Somerset County into the Great Swamp National Wildlife Refuge. So far, the state game and wildlife commission officially maintains that there are no panthers in New Jersey (and haven't been for over two hundred years), yet each year, eyewitness accounts continue to accumulate. Following the reports, however, reveals an unusual statistic: only half the sightings claim the appearance of the tawny-colored variety of panther, i.e., the North American cougar or mountain lion (*puma concolor*) that once inhabited the state. The other half are of black panthers or jaguars (*panthera onca*), the natural territory of which extends from the Florida Everglades to South America, between 1,300 and 3,000 miles from New Jersey! Are people seeing a two-species invasion of the state, or could it be something else reappearing after centuries of absence?

Today, stories of people who adopt panther cubs only to set them in the wild when they grow up and become too hard to handle or bankrupt zoos releasing their animals when they can no longer afford to house them are the stuff of urban myths. But panther folklore is, in fact, a very old American tradition, one that was adopted by white settlers from the Native Americans in every part of the frontier. In the eastern United States, there was believed to be two varieties of panthers. The first is the dangerous predator we're all familiar with that lurks in the woods and ambushes its prey from high stones or trees. The second is more elusive but no less dangerous, perhaps even more deadly. This is the Water Panther, so called because it actually lives in rivers and streams. It's the same size as a regular cougar—equipped with the same arsenal of claws and fangs as one also—but is completely black in color. Its purpose is far beyond that of a natural predator, for Water Panthers are the spirits of war that were invoked by the Lenapes during times of conflict. They are dangerous creatures in both the physical and intellectual sense, but if approached properly, it's said that a supplicant can glean great wisdom from them.

Unfortunately, I don't know what that wisdom could be or what the supplication process entails. Most Lenape rituals involved purification in a sweat lodge, specific and elaborate dances and the burning of tobacco, which was used as incense. However, approaching panthers—both the natural and supernatural kind—is not something I'd recommend for anyone to attempt. So far the alleged encounters with panthers in New Jersey haven't resulted in injuries or death, and let's hope it stays that way. But if the encounters continue to rise, it will only be a matter of time before conclusive proof emerges of the panther's return to the state. Such proof for the water variety will probably always be out of our grasp. It seems, though, judging by some of the sightings, that we may not be far from the Water Panther's reach.

If you want to see what New Jersey was like before interstates, turnpikes, chain megastores and huge corporate complexes, the rolling farmlands along Old Yorke Road in Branchburg Township and along Amwell Road in Hillsborough Township of western Somerset County would be hard to beat. There the historic lanes pass though miles of fields and farmlands lined by wooden fences, old church steeples are still the tallest buildings of the little settlements dotting the countryside and you'll probably meet more livestock than people as you drive through these towns. You might also see the Light Serpent, but don't look for it along the roadsides—you'll have to look up.

For the last 190 years, people have reported an unusual creature in the skies above this region, an airborne serpent that appears to be composed entirely of light. First seen near the Delaware River between Lambertville and McConkey's Ferry (present-day Titusville) in the 1820s, the Light Serpent appeared for several consecutive nights, baffling all who laid eyes

Above: Bodies of water are said to be the homes of Water Panthers, the Lenape demigods of war and conflict. The photo is of the Middle Brook at Washington Valley Park, Bridgewater. *Author's collection*.

Left: The Marquis de Lafayette (1757–1834), during his grand tour of the United States in 1824–25. He is said to have been one of the first witnesses of the Light Serpent. *Courtesy Library of Congress*.

on it. The Marquis de Lafayette was said to be one of the first witnesses during his grand tour of the United States in 1824–25. Following its initial sighting, the creature has been seen again well into the late twentieth century throughout the countryside between the Raritan and Delaware Rivers, encompassing Somerset, Hunterdon and Mercer Counties. Naturally, the creature's appearance causes a great commotion among those who see it, although it's reported that the serpent doesn't interact with the observers in any way. Unlike the Giant Worm, its purpose is unknown, as are its ability to fly and the reason behind its composition of light. Some people have attributed its appearance as a harbinger of misfortune; however, the events that followed—such as an earth tremor in Pennsylvania and the death of Jacqueline Kennedy Onassis in New York City—are vague or disconnected from the Light Serpent.

The possibilities behind this creature are as wide and speculative as you can imagine. Could it be an unusual astronomical event, a UFO, a hoax or misinterpretation or an actual animal? Today, through remote-controlled craft, fiber optics and even lasers, one could reproduce such an image; it would be an elaborate hoax, but one certainly within twenty-first-century means. However, attempting such a fraud in the early nineteenth century, when the only airborne objects were kites, fireworks and large balloons, would seem impossible to fool anyone but the exceptionally gullible. An optical illusion can't be discounted, either, although its appearance has been reported in several widely spread and diverse locations, which would seem to discredit environmental factors for its appearances. However, if we go back far enough into history, there may be an explanation for it.

Among Native Americans, there is a tradition of the feathered serpent—an iridescent snake god capable of flight. The most well-known form of this god is Quetzalcoatl of the Mesoamerican peoples of ancient Mexico. However, the feathered serpent was a belief that extended far from there, stretching through the Mississippi and Ohio Valleys and into the eastern seaboard of the present-day United States. Its purpose also changed with distance. Whereas Quetzalcoatl was regarded among the Mayans and Aztecs as the giver of civilization and may be linked to an actual historical figure, the feathered serpent of the North American peoples was thought of as a guardian of the skies, locked in a perpetual cold war with the demigods of earth (such as the Giant Worm) and water (the Water Panthers) to maintain the order of creation. Contrary to the belief of some Westerners who thought it was a harbinger of tragedy, the appearance of the feathered serpent was considered benevolent by the Algonquins, although getting

The Sourland Mountains looking west from Neshanic Cemetery, Amwell Road, Hillsborough. From this point to the Delaware River, sightings of the Light Serpent have been reported since the 1820s. *Author's collection.*

too close to it was believed to be dangerous. Like all supernatural beings, humans took their lives in their hands when in its presence.

Could it be that what people have been seeing for the last couple of centuries are more than just the occasional appearances of weird monsters, but in fact glimpses of a supernatural order designed to keep the world in balance? The belief system of Native Americans is vastly complex, and this triumvirate among serpents, serpent-like creatures and panthers represents only one part of that belief. However, the Lenapes believe that the natural and supernatural worlds occupy the same space but in different dimensions, rendering them invisible to each other the majority of the time. On occasion, though, the dimensions blur, making contact possible. Though this is a belief steeped in faith and religion, based on thousands of years of oral tradition, perhaps there was some physical basis for it. Perhaps the Lenapes were on to something that we're just beginning to see for ourselves.

13

RED EYES

BEDMINSTER TOWNSHIP

When I was growing up, I lived adjacent to the sixteenth green of the Warrenbrook Country Club in Warren Township, Somerset County. During the winters, when there were no golfers to bother us on our adventures, my brother, the two neighbor boys next door and I would trek through the woods to go sledding there. One afternoon in 1973, after a fresh snowfall, the four of us broke onto the green with our Flyers only to discover that someone—or something—had been there before us that day. We were good trackers for little kids, knowing the difference between the prints of deer, dogs, raccoons and humans, but these tracks were entirely new to us. What struck us about them wasn't just their large size—they were almost as long and wide as snowshoes—but that each footstep was spaced nearly four feet apart and contained five very distinct, splayed toe prints. It didn't take us long to realize that there was only one thing in the world that would walk barefoot and upright through the snow and leave such prints. Our eyes and mouths grew wide as we realized the enormous discovery we had stumbled on that day on our sleigh grounds.

Since the golf course was constructed on the northern slope of the First Watchung Mountain, we easily saw that the tracks started down near the clubhouse and went as far up the slope as we could see, leading to the promontory of the mountain at Washington Rock, which had once been a Revolutionary observation post. We decided to follow the tracks, but no sooner had those words left our mouths than the next thought entered our heads: What were four little boys going to do if they actually met the thing that made those footprints? Even my seven-year-old brain knew the answer to that couldn't end well for us, and we simultaneously bolted for home. For weeks afterward, my dreams were filled with huge shadowy beasts, and I had to be especially vigilant when roaming through the forest to make sure that the thing that made those tracks had not returned to stalk us.

None of us ever saw those tracks again on the golf course or what made them, but that is my closest encounter with the creature known worldwide as Bigfoot, the seven- to nine-foot-tall, six- to eight-hundred-pound ape-man covered from head to foot with hair that has been reported throughout North America, from Alaska to Florida and from Quebec to southern California. Except that we don't call it that in New Jersey. In the Garden State, it goes by a name that was first used by the colonists who heard of it from the Lenapes or happened to see it for themselves: Red Eyes. Granted, that name isn't as marketable as Bigfoot, which was coined by twentieth-century newspaper reporters covering Sasquatch encounters in the Pacific Northwest, but there is a logical reason the creature was called that by the colonists. It's based on the color its eyes shone at night—mostly red, but sometimes orange—which led some colonists to give him the even more awkward name of Orange Eyes. Either color is highly unusual for animal eyes to shine; most animal eyes reflect yellow and some blue, but very few in the red color range. For the colonists and the Lenapes, the color that the creature's eyes shone had an added dimension that made it more fearsome. They believed that a creature's intent could be determined by the color of its eyes, and orange or red portended the most evil of intentions. It's something that's still with us today—after all, how many horror films have you seen where the monster has purple eyes? Nevertheless, the name Red Eyes stuck in New Jersey, even if the creature didn't.

After the colonial period, sightings of Red Eyes in New Jersey evaporated, even though reports of our other monsters—like the devils, lake monsters and weird serpents—continued unabated. However, if the hypothesis that Red Eyes is a true biological creature is correct, as most who study it believe, there would be a ready explanation for its absence in the nineteenth and most of the twentieth centuries. During this time, New Jersey was completely transformed, and not completely for the better. The forests were cleared for agriculture, the waterways tamed first for gristmills but later for industrial production and the wildlife that once existed here nearly vanished, as did any large predator dependent on those resources. Ironically, though, it may have been suburbanization that allowed Red Eyes to return to New Jersey. As the farms gave way to middle-class housing, and the industrial sites were cleaned up, the forests and its wildlife returned with a huge resurgence. It may be hard to believe, but there are actually more trees, more edible plants, more deer, bears, geese and wild turkeys living in New Jersey today than at any time since the eighteenth century. We even have a whole new species of predator—the eastern coyote—that never existed before the 1990s. Sporadic reports of Red Eyes's return began in the late 1890s, long before the appearance of the coyote, but it wasn't until the 1970s and 1980s that these reports began to escalate. And when they did, one of the weirdest encounters with the creature was recounted.

Off U.S. Route 202 between the towns of Far Hills and Bernardsville in Somerset County is a narrow country lane that will take you into a deep hollow to a crescent-shaped body of water called Ravine Lake. It's a mysterious place, filled with many legends and paranormal activity. It's also one of those places that many who have lived in Somerset County their entire lives have heard about but that relatively few have been to. One late afternoon in 1986, a husband and wife had driven into the hollow and promptly became lost on one of the many side roads that branch off the main lane, which is not hard to do for first-time visitors. Stopping their car in the middle of the road, since the roads are too narrow to pull over, they tried to get their bearings. They had not been parked for long when both noticed through the car's rearview mirror something was approaching them from behind.

It was a giant silhouette of an upright creature, walking slowly on two legs toward the car. It appeared to have only one long, haired-covered arm dangling along its trunk, but the color of its hair was so dark that all other details about its appearance were obscured. Stunned by what they were seeing, the husband and wife could only stare at the creature through the rearview mirror, too frozen to even turn around and look directly at what was coming toward them.

The thing with two legs and one arm finally reached the car. It stood for a moment, then bumped the rear of the car with its hip and slowly made its way back down the road from where it emerged. The couple remained speechless in the car for several more minutes after the encounter. Finally, the husband started the engine and began driving down the road. They eventually returned to the highway, but it wasn't until they were away from Ravine Lake that they broke their silence.

"Did you see that?" he calmly asked his wife.

"Yes, I did," she answered. "But did that thing have a head?"

Throughout their entire sighting, neither could recall noticing a head on the creature. Although the creature appeared as a silhouette to them, they

Ravine Lake, Bernards Township, where a couple had a strange encounter with a crippled Red Eyes in 1986. *Author's collection.*

both believed they should at least have seen the outline of its head as it came toward them, but the top of its body seemingly ended at its shoulders. In retrospect, however, they came to believe that the Bigfoot might have had a dislocated shoulder that forced one of its arms to wrap around its head, obscuring it, which would also explain why they only saw one arm dangling from its side. The fact that it struck their car might explain how it got its injury also, but car thumping is not an altogether unknown activity of the New Jersey Red Eyes—similar incidents occurred in Morristown National Historical Park in 1966 and at Fort Nonsense in Morristown in the late 1930s, both sites lying at a distance of three and eight miles from Ravine Lake, respectively. Though New Jersey drivers have been able to hit every other type of life with their cars, there has never been a report of a run-over Bigfoot. No one can be blamed for not reporting that kind of incident, however—try explaining that to an insurance company.

Though the couple's story of a crippled Sasquatch is unusual, it is by no means the only story of such sightings in the mountains of New Jersey. Although many might be attributed to misidentification of known wildlife, particularly black bears, which have also seen a large population boom in this time period, there are enough sightings by people who know the difference between bears and huge humanoids and enough large footprints left behind

to keep this mystery going. I'm not going to write about all those incidents—those have already taken up a couple of books—but I can tell you that based on the majority of sightings in New Jersey, it appears that there is a particular migration route that the creatures follow. In the book *Monsters of New Jersey*, authors Loren Coleman and Bruce G. Hallenbeck mention a hypothesis by the late anthropologist Dr. Warren L. Cook in which he stipulates that the migration route of Bigfoot begins in Vermont and runs south through New York into New Jersey.

Once this migration route reaches the Garden State, it starts in the northwest corner of the state in Sussex County and continues one hundred miles south-southeast through Morris County, over the First Watchung Mountain in Somerset County (near my encounter when I was seven years old) and doesn't terminate until reaching the Pine Barrens of Burlington County. It doesn't necessarily follow waterways or mountain ridges (in fact, it runs counter to them), but it does follow greenways and less-developed areas in which a creature can travel with minimal or no human contact and also follows the approach and retreat of cold weather throughout the year, with the majority of New Jersey sightings taking place in the late fall and winter.

Of course, I know what you might be thinking. How can an eight-foot-tall ape-man go through the most densely populated state in the Union without being discovered? Or you might be thinking that since New Jersey is home to a lot of practical jokers that some of them are dressing up in gorilla costumes and fabricated boots and leaving footprints in the woods. It's very likely that not every reported incident with Red Eyes is genuine. Perhaps a few are outright hoaxes, too. But if you think that every single encounter is faked, I would suggest that you take a hike, literally. Go to the Watchung Reservation, where large mysterious footprints were photographed on one of the walking trails as late as 2013, or the Great Swamp, where some kind of Bigfoot-related activity has been reported almost annually since the 1970s, or Allamuchy Mountain State Park in Sussex County, which appears to be a particularly favorite destination for the creature, and start walking

Green River Road in the Great Swamp, one of the most paranormal roads in central New Jersey. First constructed by the Continental army in 1777 and only recently paved, this has been the scene for sightings of Red Eyes, the Great Swamp Devil, Yagoo, the Headless Hessian and the Sentinel, not to mention the mysterious lights of New Jersey. *Photo courtesy of Charles Kelemen.*

around. Get a feel for the forest. Notice how quickly a large buck or black bear can surprise you, and you might get an idea that something even larger than them could be living in there, too. Imagine trying to walk around in any of those locations dressed in a heavy ape costume with cumbersome Bigfoot tracks on your feet and you might realize how torturous and stupid that kind of practical joke would be to pull off. But don't worry. Chances are that Red Eyes will see you long before you see him, and he'll want to keep it that way. However, if you catch sight of red eyes shining at you from the forest depths or find a trail of huge footprints tracking along the paths, you might want to remember what a group of boys found many years ago on a golf course in winter and run in the opposite direction.

For a more complete listing of Bigfoot encounters in New Jersey, consult Coleman and Hallenbeck's book, as well as Bigfoot in New Jersey *by W.R. Matts, which contains a very weird (and unverified) story about Bigfoot and the Doris Duke estate in Hillsborough Township, Somerset County.*

PART III
THE WEIRD STUFF

14

THE PLUCKEMIN ORBS

PLUCKEMIN, BEDMINSTER TOWNSHIP

The Hills housing development in Pluckemin, Bedminster Township, Somerset County, is a textbook example of suburban sprawl. Literally covering the entire western face of Schley Mountain, the multitude of homes, condominiums and shopping centers hides secrets both below and above the surface, secrets historical and paranormal. During the Revolution, Schley Mountain was home to the Pavilion, the first military academy of the Continental army. Here Henry Knox taught Continental artillery officers to use cannon. George Washington held several celebrations there for birthdays and milestone achievements of the country's progress. If you're lucky, you might still find Revolutionary artifacts that wash down the brooks along the mountain after a rain. If you're unlucky, you might catch sight of the blue orbs that fly and dance over the summit of the mountain. That's not just a local fright—those orbs once provided the inspiration for an event that terrified the entire nation.

The concept of strange airborne objects may seem like a modern idea. Our technology and imaginations have evolved to a point where that concept is now plausible, even if the evidence for it is scant. But it is, in fact, an extremely ancient phenomenon, and the orbs of Pluckemin may be among the oldest. Over six thousand years ago, a band of Native Americans established a village on Schley Mountain, near what is now the Washington Valley Road entrance to the Hills. These people weren't Lenapes (they were still a few millennia into the future), but they were among the first humans to inhabit the area that would become Pluckemin following the great melt of the last ice age. Back then, the north branch of the Raritan River was an unimaginable torrent, sending enough debris south to form the Sourland Mountains twenty miles away. All the summits and ridges of the mountains nearby were islands or archipelagos of a great lake called Glacial Lake Passiac. It must have been an incredible new world to those first New Jerseyians, but whereas Nature had allowed them to enter that region, Super Nature drove them out.

Shortly after establishing their village, the Native Americans began to be plagued nightly by large blue orbs that emerged over the summit of Schley Mountain from the east. These orbs would streak over the treetops at an unnatural speed, stop in midair and then change direction and streak in a different way. Sometimes, they hovered in meadows and clearings, performing strange maneuvers that would lead anyone to believe that they were intelligently guided. Their sizes seemed to vary, from as small as beach balls to as big as Volkswagen Beetles, but all were the same luminescent blue as the flame of a stove gas burner, a level of heat that humans beings at that time had never seen. Those Native Americans eventually abandoned the mountainside to seek out a less troublesome place to live, but their story persisted and was handed down to future visitors to Schley Mountain. The story of the orbs might have remained only a barely remembered tale of a lost early people had not those who heard the tale seen the orbs for themselves.

To the Lenapes, the orbs were another of a host of ethereal lights that inhabited the region of Schyickbi, which is what they called New Jersey. These lights varied greatly in size, color and behavior, but nearly all were regarded with fear. The locations they were spotted in were avoided. When European colonists began to arrive in the seventeenth century, it didn't take them long to encounter the lights also, particularly those of Schley Mountain. Because of the fertile fields and plentiful water around Pluckemin, the area was irresistible to colonial farmers, who were not going to be scared off the land by the weird lights that paid visits to them in the night. In fact, during the colonial period, the orbs became known as the Mother Preakness Lights, named after an alleged witch who lived in Summit, twenty miles to the east. It was believed that the spirits of Mother Preakness and her coven would take flight from Summit and perform their rituals in the fields of Schley Mountain, which accounted for the strange, dancelike movement of the orbs. Unlike their sisters in New England, witches enjoyed a semblance of tolerance in colonial New Jersey, the alleged witch trial of Mount Holly in 1730 notwithstanding, which was actually a hoax perpetrated by none other than Ben Franklin himself. As long as the orbs didn't seem to affect the crops,

Schley Mountain, Pluckemin, Bedminster, site of mysterious orbs that have appeared there for the last six thousand years. *Photo courtesy of Peter and Rosemary Haynes.*

livestock or people in a negative manner, the colonists put up with them, although it's probably safe to assume that a lot of prayers went up from the churches in town then just to keep it that way.

The changes to Schley Mountain and Pluckemin over time didn't appear to affect the presence of the lights. They were seen again during the Revolution, when the sleepy village bloomed into a large military town with thousands of soldiers, camp followers and prisoners of war. Even the constant artillery drills didn't stop them from coming, and after the war, when Pluckemin returned to a quiet little hamlet, they remained there as well. For the next century and a half, the orbs returned over the summit of the mountain, whizzing through the sky and performing their otherworldly ballet in the fields, uncomfortably accepted by the townspeople and dismissed by those who wouldn't accept their possibility until someone whose credibility couldn't be doubted saw them for himself.

While his new estate was being built in East Amwell Township, Hunterdon County, about twenty miles southwest of Pluckemin, Charles Augustus Lindbergh—arguably the most famous man of his time for his 1927 solo flight across the Atlantic—frequently flew over Schley Mountain on the final approach to the estate's private airfield. One evening, while coming in for a landing there, the orbs appeared for Lindbergh over Schley Mountain. He reported the same phenomenon that people had been seeing for the last six millennia: blue, luminescent orbs flying at incredible speeds and performing aerial acrobatics impossible for the technology of the time. Now, Lindbergh may have entertained some wrong-headed ideas about racial superiority, but as a pioneering aviator, he knew what was supposed to be in the sky and what wasn't—these orbs definitely fell into the latter category. As an international hero, his credibility wasn't questioned, but trying to investigate and prove what these orbs were turned out to be elusive. However, the mystery of the Pluckemin orbs soon waned for Lindbergh and the rest of the country, for it wasn't long after his sighting that his toddler son disappeared from his East Amwell estate in 1932, diverting everyone's attention from this early UFO encounter.

Well, almost everyone. A few years after Lindbergh's sighting, a young man of ingenious artistic talent became fascinated by the orbs after spotting two of them for himself while staying in the Somerset Hills. He wasn't in the area searching for them; like many artists, he had a drinking problem, and he was there to dry out. However, as many artists discover, inspiration can come from the most unlikely places at the most unlikely times, and the orbs ignited his imagination. At first, the orbs didn't inspire him in an artistic sense. He actually wanted to capture one and tried to develop a trap to snare an orb. The trap was little more than a large, spring-loaded butterfly net. As his sobriety increased, even he saw the impracticality of such a device to catch an orb, so he turned his fascination with them toward something more suited to his temperament and talent. And that was how, on Halloween eve 1938, Orson Welles and the Mercury Theatre, with their radio broadcast of H.G. Wells's *War of the Worlds*, scared the entire nation into believing that Martians had invaded New Jersey and were obliterating everyone in their path. By making the broadcast appear to be actual news reports of the Martian attack, Welles achieved not only a new genre of horror but also created a classic case of mass hysteria, and it all started with those blue orbs flying over Pluckemin.

But the question remains after six thousand years: What are the orbs? Are they a natural phenomenon that we don't yet understand? Are they intelligent spirits or even life forms carrying out a purpose known only to themselves? Are they aliens or alien technology? I strongly doubt that last possibility—you'd think that, after six thousand years, aliens would have invented different ways of manifesting themselves on Earth, and no witness

Above: Charles Augustus Lindbergh (1902–1974), who had his own encounter with the Pluckemin orbs in the early 1930s. *Courtesy Library of Congress.*

Left: Orson Welles (1915–1985), whose own light encounter in the Somerset Hills helped inspire his famous *War of the Worlds* radio broadcast in 1938. *Courtesy Library of Congress, Prints & Photographs Division, Carl Van Vechten Collection, reproduction number, LC-USZ62-54231.*

has ever claimed that the orbs were ever anything but big blue balls of light. The second idea about the origins of the orbs—that they're spirits or life forms—is pretty fascinating. We now know that many animals have their own versions of self-luminescence; most of these exist beyond our visible range and can only be detected by shining ultraviolet light on them, but we have yet to explain a life form composed of what appears to be pure energy such as the orbs seem to be.

It would seem that the possibility that the orbs are a natural occurrence might hold the most logic. Pluckemin is not the only location on the planet where mysterious lights have been spotted on a regular basis. Similar light anomalies have been seen in such places as Marfa, Texas, in the 1990s and western North Carolina around the Brown Mountain region in the Appalachians up to the present day, both of which remain unexplained. One hypothesis about their origins is that they are a form of plasma energy generated by plate tectonics. One thing is certain, however: There is still a lot of weird stuff we don't know about the world we live on. After all, we didn't even know about green lightning in storm clouds until 2012 when astronauts observed it while orbiting the Earth. Maybe one day we'll figure out the orbs. I don't think their explanation will make them any less weird than they already are. They'll still inspire awe and fascination and even fear, but isn't that what life in New Jersey is all about anyway?

15

THE LIGHTS

GREAT SWAMP NATIONAL WILDLIFE REFUGE, SOMERSET COUNTY

At one time or another in our lives, we've all seen a strange light in the sky—something that doesn't fit into our initial expectations of what should be in the air. Most of the time, however, if we watch it close enough, we'll probably realize that it's really nothing unusual, even if it is uncommon. Perhaps it's an airplane or helicopter seen from an odd angle, or maybe it's a satellite in low orbit, a rocket launch or a very close encounter with a meteor. Sometimes, though, it's none of them. Don't worry—your reason isn't failing you. You've just entered the realm of the weird lights of New Jersey, and you have lots of company.

For millennia, in all parts of the state, people from all walks of life have told of strange lights appearing from the darkness. From some of the first peoples who entered the land that would become New Jersey over six thousand years ago, to the sightings that are still reported today, the lights are our most enduring paranormal phenomena, and the one that has always defied explanation. That doesn't mean attempts to explain them haven't been tried. In fact, the Lenapes and the Dutch colonists of the seventeenth century first categorized them by shape, color, behavior and consequence. Though both peoples came from vastly different worlds, they shared a similar belief in the lights and their purpose and came to the same conclusion: Most of the lights didn't bode well for the witnesses who saw them.

What follows is a breakdown of the lights according to this tradition, given to me by the great Native American folklorist Jack Rushing of the Great Swamp Folklore Project. In general, there are no particular locations where these lights have been reported—they can occur anywhere at any time—but I will mention some locations where certain kinds of light have been seen, just in case you're curious enough to check them out for yourself. I'm giving you fair warning: Some of these encounters can be truly terrifying, with permanent repercussions, such as you never being seen alive again. With that written, here are the Lights of New Jersey.

The most common—and most benign—are the white lights. These shimmering balls of energy vary in size, but all tend to be larger than the spirit orbs purportedly captured on film or video during paranormal investigations. There's controversy regarding spirit orbs among investigators, since insects, dust and other everyday particles in the air can appear to be orbs on video, but the white lights reported throughout the state are unmistakable due to their size and the fact that they give off their own light—you can picture them like disembodied searchlights or headlamps that illuminate in a full circle around themselves. Since white was the color of purity to both the Lenapes and the Dutch, these lights were considered to have a special benevolence, even called angelic by some witnesses. The color also corresponded to the colonial use of white candles to ward away evil. Although to some that might smack of witchcraft, it is in fact a practice that crosses multiple cultures and time periods, and many colonists held on to such ancient beliefs that far predated Christianity. Considering that these lights were seen by both Christian colonists and Great Spirit–worshipping Lenapes, religious affinity doesn't seem to be a requirement for their appearance. Perhaps, like the rest of the illuminations we'll visit, their meanings are colored by what the witnesses themselves bring to the encounters.

Speaking of bringing things to light-encounters, should you ever see a yellow light, you might want to have a shovel handy. It's said that their appearances mark where valuables are buried—whether this is actual treasure, a natural commodity or an object that once held some meaning for its original owner is never made clear. Sometimes the yellow light is also seen as a pillar of fire, which is believed to mark the sites of old homesteads that might still hold a long-forgotten bag of money or discarded artifacts that might now have some monetary value.

However, a shovel would be useless for the lights that progress up the spectrum from this point. Your best tools would be the white candle of the Dutch and a fast car, especially if you come against a blue light. Though the shading of these orbs can vary from light blue to violet, all are a portent of approaching evil and malevolence. These lights, which have been seen both at ground level and high in the air, are the second-most-common lights

My brother, Peter Haynes (left), examining an abandoned house in the Sourland Mountains Preserve, Hillsborough. Such abandoned homesteads are said to be marked by pillars of yellow light. *Author's collection.*

reported next to the white variety and are the kind most often reported as unidentified flying objects. As written elsewhere, these lights have been seen at Schley Mountain in Pluckemin, but they have also been reported at Lake Wanaque and Ringwood Manor in Passaic County. However, they aren't confined to these areas; they've been seen from the Hudson Highlands to the Pine Barrens, singly and in groups. In many instances, they are thought of as a ball of lightning or as actual spirit manifestations. Whatever their true nature is, though, nothing good is said to come from their appearances. Given the tragedy that happened to Charles Lindbergh's son and the eventual trajectory of Orson Welles's career after each man had his own blue light encounter, there may be something to that belief.

Whereas blue lights portend the coming of evil, red or orange lights actually are evil. These are the jack-o'-lanterns and the will-o'-of-wisps when these things were evil objects and not just holiday decorations. These are the lights that want men's lives, that appear in the woods and marshes to trick people into believing that other humans are in the wilderness with them and lead them to doom. Originally a Dutch superstition, the early colonists brought this belief with them to New Holland, only to discover that the glowing red orbs were as ensconced here as they were in Europe. When bodies of colonists were recovered from remote or inaccessible locales with no visible signs of attack or trauma, much less a logical reason why they would have been there in the first place, the orbs were blamed for their destruction. While it's said that a lighted white candle is strong enough to ward off the red lights and prevent the traveler's doom (it would also illuminate any pitfalls or traps on the path, too), it is completely powerless against the last of the mysterious orbs.

As if jack-o'-lanterns wanting your life wouldn't be bad enough, the green light wants everything—your body, mind and soul. It will even destroy your relationships should you survive an encounter with it, which, given the extraordinarily slim chance of that, may not be something to worry about too much. Sometimes, these lights are said to possess a voice capable of shattering your will, although it's unclear what it actually says, but usually its most powerful weapon is to make you completely vanish. In the days before colonization, such a triangular-shaped green light was believed by the Lenapes to reside in the woods surrounding what is today the campus of Watchung Hills Regional High School in Warren Township, Somerset County. The light would hover close to the ground, seemingly unaware of those who tried to sneak up to it to get a closer look, only to dart on the hapless victim and make them vanish in an instant. Whatever the fate was for such an unfortunate person couldn't even be speculated—they were simply gone, forever. The green light didn't confine itself to human victims, either, for it was said to take wildlife as well. What the green light was, or still is, is unknown, but one thing is certain: it wants all life that comes within its orbit.

These are the traditional lights that have plagued New Jerseyians for thousands of years. However, with the advent of our technological age, there have been additions to this list, and the numbers of their sightings, if they are to be believed, have surpassed the appearances of the old lights. These are the silver, chrome or multicolored lights, all of which have been lumped together as alien technology—in other words, UFOs. They have appeared on an almost weekly or monthly basis all over the state in remote locales, in highly populated areas and over the ocean visible from the shore. Ravine Lake, Lake Wanaque and the Clinton Reservoir have been hotbeds for these sightings since the 1960s. They are frequently reported in the skies over northeastern Middlesex County from South Plainfield to Woodbridge and are also believed by some to be responsible for the mysterious booms heard emanating from the Atlantic Ocean that have been audible from nearly every town along the coast. Unlike the traditional lights, these orbs don't

The Old Mill Dam along the Millstone River in Rocky Hill. In 1782, George Washington and Thomas Paine collected methane bubbles, a common explanation for the mysterious lights, seeping from the river. Paine believed the bubbles were responsible for the debilitating "camp fever" of the troops, but his results were inconclusive. *Author's collection.*

hug the ground but rather are reported higher in the atmosphere, at aircraft level or above. Of course, in one of the most heavily trafficked areas on the planet for aircraft, both military and civilian, many of these sightings could be attributed to misidentification. I had my own experience with that around the time of the Gulf War in 1990–91. For several very clear evenings from the Wagner Farm on Mountain Avenue in Warren Township, I distinctly saw a dark, triangular-shaped craft flying high in the sky, traveling west to east. I didn't quite know at first what I was seeing, but it wasn't long after these sightings, after the bombardment of Iraq started, that I surmised that what I had seen were F-117 Stealth Fighters on their way to the Middle East.

Well, so much for my close encounter, I thought at the time. Three years later, however, that would change.

For those who were around then, the winter of 1993–94 was a season not soon forgotten. With eighteen major snowstorms from December to March, it was one of the most crippling winters in recorded history, only surpassed by the winters of 1780–81 and 1887–88, respectively. It was during one of the frigid lulls between storms in January 1994 that I had a chance to attend my first séance conducted in Chatham Township, Morris County, by renowned psychic Jane Dougherty. Jane is a nationally recognized medium who has appeared numerous times on television. In my time, I've run across many claiming psychic abilities, most of those proving dubious at best and fraudulent at worst. Jane, however, falls into the small category of having genuine prescience; she will not ask leading questions that would cause you to divulge answers to your own questions, she reports verifiable information without any outside influences and she has a peculiar physical manifestation she undergoes when in the presence of spirits—her midsection will visibly swell to an enormous proportion and turn solid. It's like watching a pregnancy manifest in nine seconds instead of nine months. Having first met her at the tours of the Wilson-Seabrook Homestead—better known as the Spy House—in Port Monmouth, Monmouth County, in 1989 and trusting her abilities, I was excited over the prospect of what the séance might hold; considering that the séance would be held in the historical area of Morristown, a small part of me had hoped that we might make contact with some Revolutionary spirits. Being my first time at such an event, however, and not knowing what to expect, I thought it best to approach it with an open mind and allow events to unfold.

To be honest, not much happened at the séance. Of the twenty people who had gathered in the annex of the Episcopal Church where it was conducted, Jane was the only person I knew. A few of the participants seemed to have made contact with departed relatives, but the dominating presence of that night appeared to have been the deceased swami of an older Indian woman who had accompanied Jane. The spirit's name sounded to me like "Bubba," but my wife tells me that *Baba* is a more common name for swamis. Through the woman, Baba wanted to give us a message of peace and friendship, and he kept appearing even as others were sensing their relatives. For my part, I can't say that I felt anything resembling an otherworldly contact during the séance—no overwhelming impressions, emotions or visions from outside my own senses. Although I in no way claim any psychic abilities, I thought that I should have at least sensed something—that is one of the main goals of a séance, isn't it? But nothing happened for me, at least then.

The séance broke up after 11:00 p.m. I stayed for several minutes to talk with Jane and some of the participants and then headed home to Warren. The most direct route took me onto Southern Boulevard through Chatham and around the eastern edge of the Great Swamp National Wildlife Refuge, where I could reach Valley Road and later King George

Road to home. The night was clear and frigid; I had a thermometer on the outside of the car I was driving at the time. It read four degrees Fahrenheit. The speed limit on Southern Boulevard, which contains many S-turns, varies between thirty-five to forty-five miles per hour; however, due to the numerous storms that winter, the road was very narrow with four- to five-foot-high walls of packed snow and ice on both sides, and I had to proceed slower than usual to negotiate it, traveling between twenty-five to thirty miles per hour. With the lateness and desolation of the hour, though, mine was the only vehicle on that road then, and I winded my way through a strange half tunnel of ice that blocked me from seeing anything along the roadsides—houses, woods, hillsides and valleys. Only the stars above the range of my headlights were visible.

About halfway along the road at its highest point above the swamp, I became aware of a singular, bright light piercing my vision through the rearview mirror. The light approached my car rapidly and then matched my speed once it got within twenty feet of my rear bumper. Believing it to be a motorcycle headlight—it was so bright through my mirrors that it was giving me a problem concentrating on the road in front of me—I intended to let the person pass me; if he wanted to crash into an ice wall that was his business, I thought. Reaching a relatively straight portion of the road, I turned on my hazard lights, slowed to a stop, rolled down my window and waved for him to pass me. But the light didn't move.

I had learned to drive on New Jersey roads and understood the profound lack of intelligence many of my statesmen exhibited behind the wheel. I waved at him again to pass me, knowing that he couldn't possibly miss seeing my arm sticking from the car window, not with the sheer brilliance of his headlight that was illuminating the ice walls encasing the road. In fact, it was noticing how lit up the immediate vicinity had become that made me begin to wonder what was behind me—the brilliance and clarity of the light was much stronger than a headlamp. Finally something struck me as I glanced at the light through the driver's side mirror, and I stuck my head through the opened window to look at it directly.

Nothing was attached to the light.

It wasn't a motorcycle or another kind of vehicle. It wasn't a searchlight or a streetlamp. It was a ball of white light, three feet or so in diameter, hovering perfectly about the same measurement above the road surface. It didn't pulsate or change in luminosity or give off heat as far as I could tell; its brilliance was uniform, illuminating equally what was behind and below as well as in front of it. Although I probably had my eyes on it for less than two seconds, time slowed for me at that instant, the way it can when you're in a dangerous situation. Whatever motivation caused it to pursue me in the first place, by stopping the car I had given it the perfect opportunity to catch me. However, the huge orb didn't react to my watching it. After it had sped up to my car, matched my speed and then stopped when I did, it now seemed to be waiting for my next move.

If you've made it this far, you know that I've experienced a few weird things in my life. I've seen, heard and been touched by spirits numerous times; I once heard the Great Swamp Devil howling from deep within the swamp along with seventy-five other people who had heard the same thing; and thanks to some reckless choices made in my youth, I've been close to death more times than I can remember. But huge, free-floating balls of energy are where I draw my line. Tearing myself from watching the orb, I floored the gas pedal of the car and sped down Southern Boulevard. I can't tell you how fast I was going at first—I wasn't keeping track of my speedometer—but I heard my car's turbo charger racing the entire length of the road. The orb's glow was still illuminating the entire area around me—I don't even remember the darkness returning until I was off the ridge. For my entire flight, I wasn't recalling what I'd heard about the lights of New Jersey or the stories of ball lightning that my grandmother had once told me had plagued some of my ancestors or my father's story of seeing a ring of lights above the road that he was driving on a few years before my birth. Undoubtedly they were probably there in my subconscious, but for those minutes of speeding, my only goal was to get away from the light.

I was traveling nearly fifty-five miles per hour when I came to the last bend in the road at the railroad crossing just before entering New Providence. Slamming my brakes, I came to a stop and got out of the car, but the light was no longer following me. In fact, I think it had stopped pursuing me before I sped down the ridge that Southern Boulevard follows around the swamp, and the remainder of my ride home was uneventful. Thinking back to that moment in 1994, as well as now twenty years later, I had to ask myself if that event really happened—how it could have happened. That night is as fixed in my psyche as any memory I have. What the giant white orb was I still can't fathom. Was it a natural phenomenon, created by the conditions of that night that I just happened to stumble into? Was it actually attracted to my car rather than me since the car was the only thing in motion in that area at that particular time? Was it some spirit manifesting itself for me? Was it even Baba following me home from the séance? Because I can't begin to understand what the light was, I suppose that I even have to consider the possibility of an extraterrestrial origin for the light. However, trying to think from that perspective, the logic of traveling light years to Earth to chase an amateur historian on a country road only to give up the pursuit is beyond me; I hardly consider myself a candidate of interplanetary interest. Whatever the orb was, I can only be certain that I was close to it—too close to it.

My accidental adventures into the paranormal certainly didn't end that night. For the sake of disclosure, I should mention that I attended my second (and, to date, last) séance six months after this incident, once again conducted by Jane Dougherty but, this time, held at the famous Red Mill in Clinton Township, Hunterdon County. There I had a profound encounter with the spirit of a man killed by Tories during the Revolution, but there were no further light anomalies. But that's another story. I've been on Southern Boulevard countless times since that night also, in all sorts of environmental conditions, but that light never returned for me—not that I really want it to. I'm not sure that another encounter with it would end the same way it did in 1994.

I'll have to leave you with this mystery because it's as far as I've gotten with it myself. Unless or until some scientific or psychic breakthrough occurs to explain what chased me that night in Morris County, this will probably remain the most unexplained event in my life, just as the rest of the lights of New Jersey have been for thousands of years for all who have encountered them.

BIBLIOGRAPHY

BOOKS

Anderson, Fred. *Crucible of War: The Seven Years' War and the Fate of Empire in British North America, 1754–1766.* New York: Vintage Books, 2000.

Beck, Henry Charlton. *The Jersey Midlands: Landmarks and Legends.* New Brunswick, NJ: Rutgers University Press, 1984.

Chadwick, Bruce. *The First American Army: The Untold Story of George Washington and the Men Behind America's First Fight for Freedom.* Naperville, IL: Sourcebooks, Inc., 2005.

Coleman, Loren, and Bruce G. Hallenbeck. *Monsters of New Jersey: Mysterious Creatures in the Garden State.* Mechanicsburg, PA: Stackpole Books, 2010.

Cooper, James Fenimore. *The Spy: A Tale of Neutral Ground.* Akron, OH: Summit Classic Press, 2012.

Cunningham, John T. *The Uncertain Revolution: Washington & the Continental Army at Morristown.* West Creek, NJ: Cormorant Publishing, 2007.

Fenn, Elizabeth A. *Pox Americana: The Great Smallpox Epidemic of 1775–82.* New York: Hill and Wang, 2001.

Fischer, David Hackett. *Washington's Crossing.* New York: Oxford University Press, 2004.

Gagnon, Claude, and Michel Meuger. *Lake Monster Traditions: A Cross-Cultural Analysis.* London: Fortean Tomes, 1989.

Grumet, Robert S. *Indians of North America: The Lenapes*. New York: Chelsea House Publishers, 1989.

Irving, Washington. *Rip Van Winkle and the Legend of Sleepy Hollow*. New York: Penguin Books, 1995.

Johnston, Eileen Luz. *Phyllis—The Library Ghost?* Newark, NJ: Johnston Letter Company, 1991.

Ketchum, Richard M. *The Winter Soldiers: The Battles for Trenton and Princeton*. New York: Henry Holt & Company, 1973.

Lee, Francis Brazley. *New Jersey as a Colony and as a State*. New York: Publishing Society of New Jersey, 1902.

Mappen, Marc. *Jerseyana: The Underside of New Jersey History*. New Brunswick, NJ: Rutgers University Press, 1992.

Martinelli, Patricia A., and Charles A. Stansfield Jr. *Haunted New Jersey: Ghosts and Strange Phenomena of the Garden State*. Mechanicsburg, PA: Stackpole Books, 2004.

Matts, W.R. *Bigfoot in New Jersey: A Garden (State) Variety Sasquatch*. Enumclaw, WA: Pine Winds Press, 2013.

McCloy, James F., and Ray Miller. *The Jersey Devil*. Moorestown, NJ: Middle Atlantic Press, 1987.

———. *Phantom of the Pines: More Tales of the Jersey Devil*. Moorestown, NJ: Middle Atlantic Press, 1998.

Miers, Earl Schenck. *Where the Raritan Flows*. New Brunswick, NJ: Rutgers University Press, 1964.

Mitnick, Barbara J., ed. *New Jersey in the American Revolution*. New Brunswick, NJ: Rivergate Books, 2005.

Moran, Mark, and Mark Sceurman, eds. *Weird NJ: Your Travel Guide to New Jersey's Local Legends and Best Kept Secrets*. New York: Barnes & Noble Books, 2004.

Nelson, Paul David. *The Life of William Alexander, Lord Stirling*. Tuscaloosa: University of Alabama Press, 1987.

Shorto, Russell. *The Island in the Center of the World: The Epic Story of Dutch Manhattan and the Forgotten Colony That Shaped America*. New York: Vintage Books, 2004.

Showman, Richard K. *The Papers of General Nathanael Greene*. Chapel Hill: University of North Carolina Press, 1986.

Snell, James P., ed. *History of Hunterdon and Somerset Counties, New Jersey*. Philadelphia: Everts & Peck, 1881.

PERIODICALS/NEWSPAPERS/WEBSITES

Alchin, Linda. "Panther Symbol: The Indigenous People of the United States." www.warpaths2peacepipes.com. Publication date unknown.

Anderson, Gerald. "Mountain Lions in New Jersey?" *Open Salon,* June 5, 2013.

Baratta, Amy. "Ghost Hunt: Old Bernardsville Library Stirs with New Spirits." *Bernardsville News,* July 22, 2011.

Burt, Nathaniel, ed. *Princeton History: The Journal of the Historical Society of Princeton* 4 (1983).

Moran, Mark, and Mark Sceurman, eds. *Weird NJ: Your Travel Guide to New Jersey's Local Legends and Best Kept Secrets* 12, 13, 24, 29, 30, 33 and 41 (1999–2013).

Rose, Alexander. "The Spy Who Never Was: The Strange Case of John Honeyman and Revolutionary War Espionage." www.cia.gov. June 20, 2008.

Wolfe, Christian G., ed. *Black River Journal* (Autumn 2002 and September/October 2005).

INDEX

Woodbridge 112
Works Progress Administration (WPA) 85

Y

Yagoo 25, 26, 28, 30

ABOUT THE AUTHOR

Michael Haynes was born in 1966 in Plainfield, New Jersey, and raised in Warrenville in Somerset County. He has been a reporter for the *Courier News* of Bridgewater and the *Somerset Messenger-Gazette* of Somerville and a contributing writer to the *Carolina/Savannah Morning News* of Bluffton, South Carolina. He is the winner of the Robert P. Kelly Award for Feature Writing from the New Jersey Press Association. He has been a volunteer for the Somerset County Park Commission and the Great Swamp Folklore Project. His writings have appeared in the *Catawba Art & Literary Journal, USCB Literary Journal, Essence of Beaufort* and *Weird NJ*. He lives in North Carolina with his wife and their Jersey wooly rabbit that thinks he's Bigfoot.

Author's photograph.
Author's collection.